Dr. Lee Ann B. Marino, Ph.D. D.Min., D.D.

A Heart God Can Use

The Journey to the Center of His Will

A HEART GOD CAN USE

The Journey to the Center of His Will

Dr. Lee Ann B. Marino, Ph.D., D.Min., D.D.

Published by:

Remnant Words

(An imprint of The Righteous Pen Publications Group)
www.righteouspenpublications.com

Unless otherwise noted, Scripture is taken from GOD'S WORD®, © 1995 God's Word to the Nations. Used by permission of Baker Publishing Group.

Scripture quotations marked (MSG) are taken from *The Message*. Copyright © 1993, 1994, 1995, 1996, 2000, 2001, 2002. Used by permission of NavPress Publishing Group.

Scripture quotations marked (KJV) are from the King James Version of the Holy Bible, Public domain.

Scripture quotations marked (AMPC) taken from the Amplified® Bible (AMPC), Copyright © 1954, 1958, 1962, 1964, 1965, 1987 by The Lockman Foundation Used by permission. www.Lockman.org

Photos are in the public domain, Pexels.com. Cover StevenStorm JUHASZIMRUS, interior, Pixabay.

Book classification: 1. Nonfiction > Religion > Christian Life > Personal Growth

ISBN: 1-940197-50-3
13-Digit: 978-1-940197-50-0

Printed in the United States of America.

God grant that we may each of us cast off
our own works of darkness, whatever they are,
however we can, and put upon ourselves
the armor of something at least
a little like light.

(Frederick Buechner, as seen on a meme)

TABLE OF CONTENTS

ACKNOWLEDGEMENTS

When I decided to write this book, I did so as inspired by Evangelist Anthony Sluzas's theme of writing "pocket books." As one who has done his editing, interior layout, and cover design for his many written works, I thought the idea of writing a small book for evangelistic outreach and sharing purposes was a great idea. Fortunately, or unfortunately (depending on how you look at it), in the process, I learned what I am good at, and what I am not – and this particular book was not meant to be a "pocket book." While I still think it's a great idea and aspire to it one of these days (Lord willing), this wasn't meant to be it.

Regardless, I thank Evangelist Anthony Sluzas (Your Place of Grace Ministries) for inspiring me to step out and try something different. Had I not had that inspiration, I wouldn't have completed this work to begin with.

I also want to thank the many people whose discussions over the years have inspired many thoughts within me. There are so many who have proven to be great encouragers to keep doing new things, because that is what makes our lives rich and spiritual insights sharp.

And to anyone else I may have forgotten, or mentioned in the past who is still around, I thank you for remaining strong.

(1)
A PERSON AFTER GOD'S OWN HEART

He must increase in importance,
while I must decrease in importance.
(John 3:30)

D o you want to be someone that God can use to transform the world? Well, maybe not the entire world, but at least what you see within your world? Are you someone who wants to make a difference?

The odds are that you probably do, but you might not know where to start. How do I know this? Because we've all gotten excited over the different campaigns and slogans that have run through church over the past ten or 20 years. We want to be a "God chaser," a "history maker," "break up with church," participate in "pack a pew Sunday," and we want to be "emerging" and "seeker friendly." Trend after trend, we try it in the hopes it will make us stand out as one who makes a difference for God. We try all these different things, but in the long run, we all ask, what difference does it make? Chasing God down for signs gets exhausting after awhile. Being a history maker seems impossible. Breaking up with church doesn't make sense. The people who pack our church pews eventually go home, and many don't return. What are we emerging to become? How do we make ourselves friendly to people who are seeking God, especially when they have questions we can't easily answer?

We can do, and try, and put forth our best efforts, but we will still find ourselves lacking if we don't understand what makes us fundamentally usable by God.

So, what makes a person "usable" by God?

Surely there are many in this world we brand as unusable for one reason or another. Maybe they don't go to church like we might want, or they don't seem to live a life we assume is spiritual or holy in nature. We decide what is not usable by God by defining what we think – and assume – is present in a person God can use. We tend to assume that if someone claims to be "saved," "born again, "God-fearing," or maybe even "churchgoing" or "religious," they have a heart God can use and are active in His service. In my situation, I work predominately with ministers or ministers-in-training – and surely, we can assume all of them have a heart God can use, right? They've been saved for a long time, are churchgoing, interested in spiritual things, and desiring to make such things their entire lives. We believe if someone has a public work that others can see, that must mean they are used by God.

As I write this, I have been a minister for over 20 years, and a devoted Christian for most of that time. For most of those years, I have done the work with ministers and ministers-in-training I spoke of a moment ago. I can testify with some accuracy that none of these public declarations mean an individual has a heart God can – or is – using at this point in their lives. All these things are a good start and can set someone on a path to which God can use them, but just because someone makes these claims does not mean the declaration has made it all the way from their head down to their heart.

Proclamations are funny things. Most of the time, I believe people do make such declarations and proclamations for good reasons. Most people who claim to be Christian do want to do right by God, and many believe they are doing right by God, as they are, to the best of what they understand according to what they've been taught. The problem comes when we realize many of our teachings do not exist to challenge our heart conditions. In fact, they do the opposite: they contrive ways to make us feel a certain way about ourselves, not even considering the root of our motives or why we do what we do. We're told a long list of dos or don'ts, with no consideration for fixing the inner being, the part of us that does things without thinking or considering their impact on others.

In the process, we get the message that our exterior actions matter more than our interior spiritual disciplines. From an early point in our walk with God in Christianity, we learn our secret "cheat sheet," the behaviors that will get us noticed most by leadership and the most public acclaim from others. We learn how to dress, wear our hair, conduct ourselves when it's time for prayer or worship, what time to be present at church, and we pick up all the exteriors: church politics, secular politics, conducts, social interactions, and style of attire and attitude, all with the intent to make those around us think we've got it "all together."

It's possible to do these things with the best of intentions and believe you're serving God the whole time. We can do all these things and never once address our heart's condition, why we are doing the things we do, or our relationship with God. Yes, our actions do matter, but we shouldn't meet them to manifest a certain respect among men. Our actions should reflect what goes on within us, the changing of our heart. That starts with our own desire to change, and that desire should come from within us.

MISJUDGING WHAT WE SEE

It's easy to measure yourself against other believers and think you should do this or that to be usable by God. Christianity is full of ministers all using this same technique, mimicking what they see popular or more established ministers do, trying it out for themselves. Sometimes their efforts work; much of the time, at least a few people will follow someone who appears to do what "works" for others. They've probably heard testimonials or other personal tributes as to what works, so they'll follow someone doing the same thing, expecting the same results. Even for those it works, those techniques eventually begin to fail. Why? Because they aren't being done out of motive, but habit. Instead of developing what God desires to bring forth from that minister to the benefit of the people, they are using a method that was for someone else.

We can apply this same logic to our own lives as we walk with God, no matter what our position in church may be. Yes, there are certainly general guidelines for all of us as believers. These things help to set us on the right path and do what we need to do in our own lives to make sure our faith grows, develops, and becomes strong. Yet there is a key to this that doesn't always happen: the push to make our faith personal. All of us can believe in God in a dry, distant manner that is about nothing more than words on a page. We can say we believe in God, we can say we have faith…but it can mean nothing more than a theory or idea that we muse about life or the afterlife.

Our walk as believers is supposed to be more than just something we do as a musing or an idea. Believing in God isn't supposed to be something we do to be good on paper or right on paper. It's also not something we do for the sake of avoiding punishment, whether now or in eternity. We do it because we are thinking about eternity; we have eternity set in our hearts; and we want to adopt that mentality to think much longer-term than the longest term thought we've ever had. We desire that unity with God, our place with Him, and that is supposed to change our heart.

This process starts when we get real with ourselves and try to judge ourselves, to see ourselves just as we are. This is not always easy, but it is necessary if we want to know we have a heart God can use.

JUDGING OURSELVES AGAINST OTHERS…IN A NOT-SO-HOLY MANNER

We're now going to have a "heart to heart" moment that is the first to challenge us as we examine ourselves. It's time for a difficult truth: the way we measure ourselves isn't often for holy purposes. It's not to get better, live right, or become better. It's to make us feel better about ourselves and where we are in our lives. It is our hope that as we judge ourselves against people who are different from us in some way, we can justify our own ways of being that are not pleasing before God.

Many years ago, I dated a man whose claim to fame was being baptized in Jesus' Name three different times. He felt because he'd been baptized three times to my one, he was superior to me in faith and in my perspectives of faith. He was quick to fall back on that argument any time we ever fought. In the beginning, what he said worked. I wondered if maybe I wasn't faithful enough because I hadn't been baptized enough. That was until one day, toward the end of our relationship, when words came out of my mouth that I had no idea were there: "Well, if you had to be baptized so many times, maybe it was because it just didn't take the first time."

Using this subject matter makes his attitude sound absurd. Of course, it doesn't make sense to think that being baptized so many times makes one more advanced in their faith. If anything, it might make one wonder why it took so many baptisms for faith to take effect! But the attitude he had was one that too many of us have about the fallings and sins of others. He was measuring what he felt he knew about me to justify where he was, and all the things and manners by which he hadn't come. In other words, he might not have been usable by God, but he certainly felt he was superior to me. No, I wasn't perfect. I still am not there. But he was no better than I was because of his multiple baptisms. He wasn't sin-free because he went to two church services a week and didn't watch television. He had no right to sit in judgment of what he felt I was doing wrong in my life. If we were to talk about sin in a serious manner or discuss our relationship as adults, that would have been one thing, but the "anything you are doing, I'm not doing better" kind of behavior is all too often used against others. It's not the way God desires us to address one another in this life.

Let's understand that God deals with each one of us individually, because each one of us sins. No matter how many days a week we spend in church and no matter how many things we do that appear churchy or right, we still sin. We might not sin every single day and we might not deliberately set out to sin once we reach a certain point in our walk, but we are deluding ourselves if we say we never sin.

If we say, "We aren't sinful" we are deceiving ourselves, and the truth is not in us. God is faithful and reliable. If we confess our sins, He forgives them and cleanses us from everything we've done wrong. If we say, "We have never sinned," we turn God into a liar and His Word is not in us. (1 John 1:8-10)

Sin is, unfortunately, a part of our lives down here. It doesn't have to be the end of the line, however. We can get so tangled up in worrying about sin and sinning that we forget to live and seek the freedom we find in Christ. Jesus has the answer for our sins in His sacrifice for us on the cross. Forgiveness is ours. We can receive it. But that doesn't mean we never sin. If forgiveness is the answer, that means sin is the problem.

This simple fact is glossed over many times by ministers who I think mean well, but really don't grasp the relevance of sin in our lives. If we are all sinners, that means we have an honest leveling ground in our lives. We all start out from the same place, and we all wind up in the same place. The only thing that makes the difference in the middle is our willingness to receive the forgiveness of God. God had to – and must – intervene on our behalf to make things right for us.

You were once dead because of your failures and sins. You followed the ways of this present world and its spiritual ruler. This ruler continues to work in people who refuse to obey God. All of us once lived among these people, and followed the desires of our corrupt nature. We did what our corrupt desires and thoughts wanted us to do. So, because of our nature, we deserved God's anger just like everyone else.

But God is rich in mercy because of His great love for us. We were dead because of our failures, but He made us alive together with Christ. (It is God's kindness that saved you.) God has brought us back to life together with Christ Jesus and has given us a position in heaven with Him. He did this through Christ Jesus out of His generosity to us in order to show His extremely rich kindness in the world to come. God saved you through faith as an act of kindness. You had nothing to do with it. Being saved is a gift from God. It's not the result of anything you've done, so no one can brag about it. God has made us what we are. He has created us in Christ Jesus to live lives filled with good works that He has prepared for us to do. (Ephesians 2:1-10)

These words are great and awesome and fill us with hope (or at least they should). They remind us that God has done something for us that is not achievable by our powers alone and should cause us to realize how much God really does love us. God has done above and beyond what He had to do transform our lives. All we must do is receive what He has provided to start that process within us. It sounds great and glorious, and a concept of spiritual eternity that should shake our reality and transform us forever. More than anything, it should be a humbling reality.

Many times, despite what God has done, we fall back on our flesh, on the very part of us that is comfortable doing things ourselves. We don't quite regard what God did for us in the same way. Sometimes we take matters into our own hands, overlooking the humility involved in receiving what God has done for us in full. We start taking judgment upon ourselves. We might protest and call it "assessment of a situation" or fight about what judgment means, but judgment is judgment is judgment. It creeps in any time we start to get a little too comfortable with ourselves and we want to avoid the discomfort that comes with proper self-judgment and examination.

We like judgment, though. Oh boy, do we like judgment. We haven't quite learned to hate sin yet, at least not in the way we should…but we love judgment. No matter how often we claim to avoid it or not want it (and we certainly dislike it when others point it in our direction), we find ourselves doing it. Have you ever wondered why this is? We love judgment because it makes us feel better about ourselves and our little mishaps.

Yes, I know, ouch. The "Hallelujah!" will come later.

I once saw a video on YouTube in which an Orthodox Jewish Rabbi spoke on the principle of love. He made the statement that self-love is something natural that comes naturally to each one of us. We can easily say we love this or that, or that we love others, but the truth is that most of the time, we love what others do for us or how they make us feel about ourselves. If we look at things through this lens, there is some truth to it. We love messages about loving ourselves in church because it echoes something we already embrace and receive for ourselves. We always want to hear more about how we should "treat ourselves good" or "do more for ourselves," because that caters to our basic nature to love ourselves. Learning about loving ourselves might make us feel good and make us feel better about things we do wrong, but it doesn't challenge us to do any better for anyone else or to be more conformed to the image God calls us to become.

Self-love exists for survival and personal preservation. Not everything about it is warped or distorted, but it is easily warped and distorted into something that justifies our personal sins and exalts us above other people. It easily becomes a weapon we use to preserve ourselves against the truth about ourselves and others. When this happens, self-love turns into something vicious by nature, something angry, something…judgmental. Something to lift me up and put you down.

We love judgment because when push comes to shove, we love ourselves. We love the reflections of ourselves in our lives, whether it's our material possessions, the size of our bank accounts, our families who share our DNA and look just like us, our friends, and our own personal self-preservation. There might be things we don't like about ourselves, or wish were different, but that is different from the principle of self-love. Judgment proves this. When it's between us and them in the natural realm, "them" is never going to win.

Stop judging so that you will not be judged. Otherwise, you will be judged by the same standard you use to judge others. The standards you use for others will be applied to you. So why do you see the piece of sawdust in another believer's eye and not notice the wooden beam in your own eye? How can you say to another believer, 'Let me take the piece of sawdust out of your eye,' when you have a beam in your own eye? You hypocrite! First remove the beam from your own eye. Then you will see clearly to remove the piece of sawdust from another believer's eye. (Matthew 7:1-5)

We know that judgment gets thrown around a lot and this passage is used in all sorts of ways, but what about judgment is so bad? Why shouldn't we judge? Why, of all things, would God make a point to tell us we shouldn't judge other people – because it will mean we will be judged? So, what if we're judged, right? Who cares what other people think! Anyone who doesn't like me is a "hater," anyway! Down with other people's opinions, right?

Wrong.

There are many things in the Scriptures that pass as interpersonal relationship issues but relate to spiritual ones in many ways. Never assume that our relationships with others have nothing to do with our relationship with God; the opposite is true. Every relationship we have is about our relationship with God. In every relationship, interaction, and experience we have in life, God teaches us things about ourselves. He is revealing to us things He wants us to know about Him, about spirituality, and yes, about ourselves. Our relationships aren't just relationships; they are training grounds. Whenever we stick judgment in the picture, we stop our training, and we start trying to play coach when we are unqualified to do so.

Being spiritual people and being aware of our different spiritual gifts and insights is a great thing, but without proper balance, those things can easily become a source of self-love instead of divine revelation of God's love to us. It's easy to say, "I can do this…and this, and this, and this!" and after awhile, God is not a part of it anymore. In judgment, we overlook important spiritual principles and spiritual flow that can help us minister to, reach out to, or better love others because we have decided there is something about them that isn't worthy of God's love or what we have to offer. If we judge them, we don't have to reach out, do anything, and we can stay right where we are, because we are "superior."

You can tell yourself all day long this isn't what is at the root of judgment, but it is. If we judge others, we can't hear from God about the right way to reach out. We can stay where we are, we can ignore our own sins, and we can be comfortable as we run around the church and proclaim our freedom. If we are still judging others, we aren't free. We are bound by our own self-love, which has led us to sin.

If we judge others, we open ourselves up to divine judgment, not just for other people to judge us. By judging others, we put ourselves in God's position, and we are unqualified to do that. The measure – standard, establishment, guide – that we use to judge others is just how God is going to judge us, but this doesn't mean the subject matter is the same. If we are unkind, God will look at us with unkindness. If we are harsh, God will look at us harshly. If we are inconsiderate, God will look at us with inconsiderateness. God knows everything about us, everything about every situation under the sun, and we do not. Sometimes things happen for reasons we do not consider, and sitting around, judging someone else's sin when we have our own, is just wrong.

What we should do is turn our judgment on ourselves, examine ourselves before the Lord, and let God show us what we need to change about ourselves…and then change it. We won't become perfect, but we will be focused on the things we need to change, who we are called to be, and how we can help and reach out to others.

How many crimes and sins have I committed?
  Make me aware of my disobedience and my sin. (Job 13:23)

Each of you must examine your own actions. Then you can be proud of your own accomplishments without comparing yourself to others. Assume your own responsibility. (Galatians 6:4-5)

Taking those first steps means we will see things we do not like within ourselves, but that shouldn't stop us from being real about who we are and the things we do wrong. If we address the truth about ourselves, God helps us, often step by step, to find our way to freedom.

FOLLOW YOUR HEART

When the Bible speaks about the heart, it talks about our inner nature, the personal desires and dialogues we have with ourselves at the essence of our being. We hear many contradictory things on the heart and the nature of the heart. The world sometimes tells us to "follow our heart" or that our "heart will guide us," but then we hear in church that the heart is decidedly and impossibly wicked…or still, that God will give us the desires of our heart. Which one is it? Talk about confusion! From one angle, it would appear the heart is good; from another, it would appear bad. It is true the Bible does speak of the heart as not being particularly good, but that is not all that is said about the heart. There is one very important thing our heart does lead us to, however, and that is the truth about ourselves. That is, if we are willing to heed and hear what it is really saying about us.

Lay not up for yourselves treasures upon earth, where moth and rust doth corrupt, and where thieves break through and steal: But lay up for yourselves treasures in heaven, where neither moth nor rust doth corrupt, and where thieves do not break through nor steal: For where your treasure is, there will your heart be also. (Matthew 6:19-21, KJV)

There are many ways people interpret this passage, but what it's trying to tell us is that whatever is most important to us can be found by following our financial priorities. In other words, whatever we love the most, that's where we spend most of our money. Whatever we love, whatever we love about ourselves, whatever expresses our personal self-love, and whatever we want most, that's where we find our money.

Following our heart's path to the truth about us (especially when we trail it through our finances) often reveals to us a very stark and grave reality about where we are in our lives and what is most important to us. See, we have learned to be good at lying, not just to the world, but to ourselves about our priorities. We hear the chants that "family should be first" (God should be first, but I digress) and that certain things should be our main priorities in life, and we know how to angle ourselves as a best possible model of the so-called values of others in our exterior positions. We are quick to gossip, judge, and look down on anyone who doesn't clean up quite as well as we do. But if we genuinely examine where our money goes, is it going where it should? Odds are good there is something, somewhere that indicates a different priority than you show to the world. Your money, and where it goes, reveals the essence of you.

If we are going to properly judge and assess our character, we must look at what we do with our money and see things in reality that we may not like. It's easy to assume we are doing the right things with our money – and our lives – if we do what we can to meet the minimum surface requirements to look right. Remember, this little crash course isn't about how to look the part; it's about how to really be the part. Often we get so comfortable with looking right, we believe our lies that we are right. If it stares us in the face in our spending, saving, hoarding, or however else we use our money, we can't deny it.

By examining ourselves, God desires us to reach a place where we can't deny these things. To get real spiritually and get right with God, we must be honest with ourselves about who we are and what we really want out of this life. In some instances, much of what we want might sound great. It might sound like what we think we should aspire to and what we should want. We don't say we want money; we say we want "financial stability." We don't say we are afraid to be lonely, we say we want a "family." We don't say we want a bigger house; we say we "need more space." We don't say we dislike people from other countries; we say we're worried about "jobs" or "security." There are a million ways we try to cover up our true wants and desires by making them sound more noble than they might be, lying not just to others, but ourselves, as well. Yes, those might be the things we want within the smaller scope of life, but the truth is that we want more money, and we want the things it buys because those things represent status to us. Behind status, we find power. If we have the money, we will have the power, and be able to control our domain, environment, those around us, and, in a general sense, our immediate world.

Statistics cite money as the one thing couples fight about more than anything else: more than children, sex, and other relationship issues, combined. More divorces ensue with money at the helm than most other issues, at least on the surface. Have you ever stopped to wonder why this is? When couples fight about money, they aren't fighting about the green ink and paper that's printed and distributed by banks; they are fighting about a concept. It is that same, inherent concept of self-love and self-desire we spoke of earlier, manifest in the form of trying to do what's perceived as right or best for oneself through financial control. Couples who fight about money aren't fighting about money; they are fighting for control and self-interest. Arguments about money are the struggle for power, to avoid being dominated and to dominate. This is why fights about money tend to be so infinitely terminating for relationships, and so damaging to those that survive. The fight isn't about money, or about how it's spent, it's about something far more serious that impacts our heart condition and the realities of what is most important to us. Because we haven't been taught to be honest about our true intentions, we don't know how to verbalize it, and financial discussions end in disagreement and disrepair.

One of the major reasons the Bible talks so much about money and encourages us to seek after things that are not financial nor material in this world is because the root of such seeks our personal stake in power and control. Through power and control, we seek to do something for ourselves that we will never be able to do. Sure, we might be able to have influence down here or appear to control our destinies, but there are just some things that money can't buy. It is certainly true we need money to survive. It is also true that many of us, if we are honest with ourselves, are looking to money for far more than survival.

A godly life brings huge profits to people who are content with what they have. We didn't bring anything into the world, and we can't take anything out of it. As long as we have food and clothes, we should be satisfied.

But people who want to get rich keep falling into temptation. They are trapped by many stupid and harmful desires which drown them in destruction and ruin. Certainly, the love of money is the root of all kinds of evil. Some people who have set their hearts on getting rich have wandered away from the Christian faith and have caused themselves a lot of grief. (1 Timothy 6:6-10)

We find our place, our grounding in this life, in contentment because we know what we have is from God. This helps us to be grateful for what we have. In some things, we just need to be still. The drive and pursuit to make money never ends, because after that comes more money, and more money still, and more to gain, with more to lose. If that's our goal – not to find ourselves content and purposed, but to keep gaining more and more and more – we are going to always find ourselves in a place that lacks contentment. The love of money is the root of all evil because the love of money comes from the heart, from the part of us that loves ourselves, puts ourselves first, looks about selfishly, and desires to compete with and destroy anyone and anything in the process that interferes with our agendas. It's the opposite of contentment. As the Bible tells us, it causes us to fall into temptation. Why? It represents a weakness, a place where the enemy can infiltrate, and we easily find ourselves separated from God.

Before you say, "This isn't me," follow the trail of your finances. What is most important to you? Where does your heart lie? Is it selfish and stingy? Is it spent on things that are not eternal? Do you have money for everything but the things of God? Do you sow into the Kingdom regularly? Is all your money gone before you know what happened to it? Does money represent something more to you than meets the eye? What are you fighting over through money with others?

Where your treasure is, there your heart is, also. The treasure doesn't lie. Neither does the heart. The heart might deceive us, it might deceive others…but it tells the truth about us, and where we are. When it comes to us, the heart absolutely does not lie.

TRADITIONS

So, if these are all things we need to examine within ourselves and all these things tell the truth about us, why aren't we aware of how loud we are speaking our truth? (Our truth being that reality which has become personal to us.) We think we're so clever, hiding it beneath the things we say and do, so much so that we don't even realize how obvious what we say has become. We've been conditioned to our world, to our comforts and our societies that encourage us to speak and behave as we do. Then we go to church, and we find ways to remain comfortable and unchallenged as we are. The way we do this is through tradition.

Before I define tradition, let's look at the difference between creating a comfortable church and a welcoming church. It's important that churches are welcoming, but that we never let anyone get too comfortable. Often churches are the opposite today – they are comfortable for some but not welcoming. This is how you can test yourself: If your church's consistent message affirms you, in your flesh, and makes you feel great and confident in yourself without challenging any of your thoughts, beliefs, ideals, or opinions, then you are attending that church because it makes you comfortable. Odds are good that with that kind of an ideal, your church is unwelcoming to someone because it has chosen to affirm your flesh over the work of the Spirit. If your church's consistent message makes you feel great and confident in how you are and never challenges any of your thoughts, beliefs, or opinions, then you are comfortable at that church, and that's a big part of why you attend every week.

If this is the case, then you, my friend, are in some way blinded by tradition.

Traditions are things done a certain way as were passed down or encouraged by someone else. No one really knows where they started or where they will end. They are handed around between people because they serve a universal purpose. Traditions absolve us from looking as deeply at ourselves as we ought. They also unite us in a special way to others who feel the same way about issues as we do. They help us gloss over our exceptions to the rules and keep us going forward, like we don't have any issues in the world.

Over the years I've been a Christian, I've noticed how quick we often judge the Catholic Church, more traditional churches, or even other churches for their traditions, all the while, ignoring our own. We all have traditions; ours are just different from someone else's. It's more obvious to say that someone has "traditions" that are obvious – such as wearing their hair a certain way, no make-up, praying to someone other than God, or specific dietary guidelines – than it is to examine ourselves and see where those traditions are within every one of us.

My own testimony involves a long-fought battle with tradition and insights into tradition. The Christian part of my testimony starts when I left the Catholic Church after what seemed like a long battle back in 1999, when I was 17. In reality, the battle raged for only about four months, but at that age, it might as well have been an eternity. There were doubts and concerns along the way, and one of the biggest issues that arose was the question of many church traditions. It was easy for me to go through my Bible and see where many Catholic traditions didn't fit. It was especially easy to walk away from many of them because there was so much out there about those traditions. It was easy to see what they were and where they were, clearly identifying the things that caused me to avoid different spiritual issues in my life.

It was relatively easy to abandon these traditions because I was ready to do so. They seemed very relevant at the time. Everyone had an opinion and reaction to my Catholic background that not only inspired questions, but it also often inspired downright disdain. I was eager to abandon those things that would cause me to stand out, not fitting in with those who I thought had "the truth." However, down through the years, I can't help but notice the number of traditions many around me have, even today. Despite this fact, I never hear about a war on the traditions we've created as our own. I'm still hearing about the evils of Catholic tradition and now the various holiness traditions that a limited number of professing Christians still follow today. For example:

- I hear about Catholics praying to Mary and to the saints, not about the way that popular television preachers are idolized and worshiped by people who buy their books, share their memes, and hold to their teachings as if they were Gospel…even in the face of their scandals, theological errors, and their lack of credentials.

- I hear about Catholic worship as stiff and rigid, but never about the way that people do the same things in worship over and over again, such as running around the room on a musical cue or drumbeat.

- I hear about priests being served on the altar by altar servers, but never about armor bearers or adjutants serving ministers.

- I hear about priestly celibacy regarded as sinful and unnatural, but never about the fact of how wrong it is for a minister to sleep with half of their congregation.

- I hear about how wrong it is for holiness preachers to harp on how long a woman's hair is or how bad it is to discourage women from wearing make-up, but we never hear about the way we shame women for wearing a shorter skirt or too much make-up.

I'm forever hearing about everyone else's traditions, and not nearly enough about our own. If we want to have a heart God can use, we must deconstruct those things that make us feel all right with where we are, who we are, and glossing over what we do that's wrong. We must start examining ourselves for real, without the safety net and comforts of personal tradition.

Then some Pharisees and experts in Moses' Teachings came from Jerusalem to Jesus. They asked, "Why do Your disciples break the traditions of our ancestors? They do not wash their hands before they eat."

He answered them, "Why do you break the commandment of God because of your traditions? For example, God said, 'Honor your father and your mother' and 'Whoever curses father or mother must be put to death.' But you say that whoever tells his father or mother, 'I have given to God whatever support you might have received from me,' does not have to honor his father. Because of your traditions you have destroyed the authority of God's word. You hypocrites! Isaiah was right when he prophesied about you:

'These people honor Me with their lips,
*   but their hearts are far from Me.*
Their worship of me is pointless,
*   because their teachings are rules made by humans.'"*

Then He called the crowd and said to them, "Listen and try to understand! What goes into a person's mouth doesn't make him unclean. It's what comes out of the mouth that makes a person unclean."

Then the disciples came and said to Him, "Do you realize that when the Pharisees heard your statement they were offended?"
He answered, "Any plant that My heavenly Father did not plant will be uprooted. Leave them alone! They are blind leaders. When one blind person leads another, both will fall into the same pit."

Peter said to Him, "Explain this illustration to us."

Jesus said, "Don't you understand yet? Don't you know that whatever goes into the mouth goes into the stomach and then into a toilet? But whatever goes out of the mouth comes from within, and that's what makes a person unclean. Evil thoughts, murder, adultery, other sexual sins, stealing, lying, and cursing come from within. These are the things that make a person unclean. But eating without washing one's hands doesn't make a person unclean." (Matthew 15:1-20)

The problem with our traditions is illustrated well in this passage, and it parallels what I spoke of a few moments ago. Tradition is constructed to make sure we don't see what's right in front of us as pertains to ourselves, because we are too busy doing something that someone came up with generations ago for us to do. As we do it, it makes us feel superior – self-righteous, self-fulfilling – of whatever purpose and duty we have as believers. Traditions keep us busy; they fill our time, our spiritual space, and distract us from true examinations. They keep us from being real about ourselves and real with God about who we are. Yes, God knows all, but it's amazing how fake we can try to be with Him. We hope He won't see through the façade our traditions help us keep in place…but He does.

The traditions upheld by the Pharisees and Sadducees appeared to be good. At least on the surface, they seemed to have some sense of Biblical nature. Neither camp might have agreed with the other's perspective of "Biblicalness," but to them, it made sense. It seemed like they had a knowledge of Scriptures. You'd think their theories would lead their followers closer to God. That's the way it is with all our traditions. They sound good; they seem good; but they create self-righteousness within us, something by which we deceive others and ourselves about just who we are and what we are about.

Instead of relying on tradition, start looking at your relationship with God differently and move by the Spirit. Tradition blocks the voice of the Spirit, but when we are aware of it, the Spirit can transform us to a point where we move and operate differently. The Spirit guides where tradition cannot, and where we have become self-righteous, we can become the righteousness of God in Christ.

RELYING ON GOD

All the things we've discussed up to this point are things that help us rely on ourselves rather than on God. One of the biggest barriers we have in our relationship with God is allowing God to work in and through us, especially unto the change that we must have to be usable by Him. This might sound like a strange topic of discussion for those who already consider themselves believers, but believing in something, in and of itself, doesn't transform a person. It's a great start, but it is entirely possible to believe in something as an idea and not allow that belief to change you in any way.

Another person might say, "You have faith, but I do good things." Show me your faith apart from the good things you do. I will show you my faith by the good things I do. You believe that there is one God. That's fine! The demons also believe that, and they tremble with fear.

You fool! Do you have to be shown that faith which does nothing is useless? Didn't our ancestor Abraham receive God's approval as a result of what he did when he offered his son Isaac as a sacrifice on the altar? You see that Abraham's faith and what he did worked together. His faith was shown to be genuine by what he did. The Scripture passage came true. It says, "Abraham believed God, and that faith was regarded as the basis of Abraham's approval by God." So Abraham was called God's friend. You see that a person receives God's approval because of what he does, not only because of what he believes. The same is true of the prostitute Rahab who welcomed the spies and sent them away on another road. She received God's approval because of what she did. (James 2:18-25)

We can believe anything that we want, anything under the sun, whether good or bad. Those beliefs will not change us if we don't allow them to do so. Even in the demonic realm, demons know who is who and what is what, and where it's at – but believing those things is simply not enough to transform them. Sure, we talk about belief – we believe this, we believe that, we are going to stand behind our belief in this or that – but when does belief transform to become more than just something we embrace as a musing or a concept? Our faith is supposed to show us who we are and Who God is. As we walk this faith thing out, we are supposed to come to a place where we learn to rely on God in a way that's often very different from what we hear about and talk about in church. Think about some of the expressions you often hear spoken by Christians:

- "Heaven helps those who help themselves."
- "Cleanliness is next to godliness."
- "Spare the rod, spoil the child."
- "Money is the root of all evil."
- "God don't like ugly."
- "Everything happens for a reason."
- "God never gives you more than you can handle."

None of these expressions are found in the Bible. In fact, most of them don't even have a Bible verse to point back to where they could be considered almost Biblical. Yet they all have something in common: they rely on our own understanding; our own concepts of belief and ideals that will help keep us – you guessed it – comfortable. They echo our inability to process or handle the things we don't like or don't understand, and we say these things to try and provide ourselves a way to rely on what we believe, even if it's not enough to truly transform where we are.

Trust the Lord with all your heart,
and do not rely on your own understanding.
In all your ways acknowledge Him,
and He will make your paths smooth.
Do not consider yourself wise.
Fear the Lord, and turn away from evil. (Proverbs 3:5-7)

Proverbs 3:5-7 is often quoted, but I don't know that we really understand what it says. This passage sums up what it means to rely on God in two verses, and the Bible overall shows us about trusting God in a bigger sense as we look over the lives of those who made that commitment to trust God all their days. If we really rely on God, we don't lean on ourselves and our own perceptions of things to get through them all the time. Relying on God is more than just believing God to get you through a bad time or to get a bill paid for you that you are unable to cover in the natural. When we truly make the effort to rely on God, we cut through everything that is us that blocks us from Him and we surrender ourselves to Him. It's a surrendering, not because we lose ourselves, but because we find a greater purpose and meaning within.

Without God, we will eventually find ourselves empty in this life. It won't matter how much money we have or how great what we do appears in the eyes of others. We will reach a point in time where what we do doesn't satisfy us anymore. It won't give us the sense of purpose we hope it will, because the reason we do it is all about us or about others around us who expect it from us. We have been created to know, love, and communicate with our God, so anything we try to do without relying on Him – on the One Who is first, last, and everything in between – is going to reach an emptying point. Sure, it might take awhile, and it might not seem so empty at first, but eventually, there will be that little part within every one of us that is looking for something more, for a connection between what we do and the bigger picture of eternity.

Whenever you learn how to use an invention or a new product, the best thing to do (especially when that product is new) is learn from the creator of the product how to use it properly. We might fumble and try to figure it out on our own, but the odds are good we won't get very far. It might seem like a fun challenge at first, but it will quickly turn into confounding and frustrating work. If we believe and recognize that God has created us, then that means we need to consult Him, our Creator, for just what to do and how to do it. In all our ways – the ways that we take on as our own – we should acknowledge Him – so He will guide our paths and make them smooth.

To find this, we must rely on God – for His purpose and His plans, for the things we go through in this life that don't seem very meaningful, the difficulties we don't understand, the things we don't always want to do, and the times that make sense – in everything, because in everything, God is speaking to and reaching out to us. Relying on God isn't a strange, weird process by which we sound deep. It does not mean we do everything perfectly or never make mistakes. It doesn't even mean that there won't be times when we miss God and His guidance in our lives. It is a practical approach to living that seeks out God for our steps and our general sense of purpose rather than running off on our own. Our thoughts and ideas might deceive us, but God will not deceive us. To be used by Him, we must know how to follow His direction and recognize His presence in our lives.

Transforming Your Heart

We all love the passages of Scripture that we interpret to mean God wants to do good things for us and that He will give us the things we want. If it's a message about getting, about receiving from God, about having the deepest things we want, of course, we love those ideas and are going to get on board with them. Are those passages saying what they think we do, or are we misinterpreting them all together?

Be happy with the Lord,
and He will give you the desires of your heart.
Entrust your ways to the Lord.
Trust Him, and He will act on your behalf. (Psalm 37:4-5)

The passage above, so often cited, isn't saying that God will just give us whatever we want...just because. It describes a needed process, also known as the transformation of our hearts.

Let's get real, for a moment (or actually, for this whole book): All of us want things. Some things we want with a passion, other things we want with less enthusiasm, and other things, we want as a passing phase or interest. From the time we are very young, we want what we want.

- If it's ours and we give it away, we want it back.
- If it's someone else's, we want it.
- If it's different from ours, we want it.
- If it looks like ours, we want it.
- If we think we might need it for something later in time, we want it.
- If someone has it on television or on the internet, we want it.

It starts young, matures, transforms, and becomes something else, entirely, the older we get. We get bored with our things because others have different things. Every time we look around us, it seems like there is something that someone else has or is trying to sell that we want. Life can be an endless process of frustration as we attempt to chase after everything we see, feel, and desire, even when we reach the point where it's not everything that we see.

How many of us are willing to admit that every time we go to get dressed, we don't "have a thing to wear?" How many of us will openly admit that every time we pass a new car, there's a part of us that looks down on the one we have? How many of us are willing to admit that whenever we hear that someone has got a new house, we're wondering how long it's going to be before we can move up, just like they did?

Then, we've learned how to do the cleverest thing imaginable: we take our wants before God and expect that He will give them to us, "just because" we saw someone else with something and that set off an entire chain of discontentment within us. We think taking it to God makes it more noble or righteous than if we just want it to want it. It's our sincere hope that taking our malcontented, wanting selves to God will change what we want into something sincere, something less...of the flesh...than it really is.

I sometimes wonder if God gets as tired of our materialistic prayers (disguised as spiritual requests) as I get of hearing about them. I've met people – some ministers, some not – who never make a request before God for anything but things. We live in a world full of need, lack, and insight, and our prayer lives reflect a desire to "keep up with the Joneses" rather than meet genuine needs that exist. Pretending we are praying with "God's will" when we haven't the least clue of what that is doesn't change the fact that we are praying for our own desires to be met...not God's.

Psalm 37:4-5 doesn't promise our endless desires are ours for the picking in the spiritual realm. Rather, it tells us to be happy with the Lord, and He will give us the desires of our heart. The first part of that phrase, what comes before receiving from God, is finding ourselves happy (or, as some translations state, delight yourself in the Lord) in Him. This means that we unite ourselves to God, transforming our hearts and their desires to the things of God. In such a place, we don't find the conflicts between the flesh and the Spirit, because we come to want what God wants for us. When our desires are the same as God's, our desires will be met. Instead of seeking God for the wrong things, then our heart's cry will be:

...*However, Your will must be done, not Mine.* (Luke 22:42)

We must set our sights properly on the very things that God desires and to pursue the right things in life, those that reflect a love that's beyond this earth and beyond ourselves. When we are willing to transform our hearts, we will be better able to obey God, because we will embrace His will as our own.

Embracing the will of God and delighting ourselves in God is more than just doing things that God tells us to do. It is looking beyond the mere standards of obedience to become one who loves God enough to deeply understand and adapt His nature within one's life. When we talk about obedience, we seldom, if ever, talk about transforming our hearts, which means that obedience will forever be a difficult task for us. If we don't gain some sense of unity with the Father, of His heart and His love toward us and His desires for us, we will always struggle with obedience, because we won't understand Him. No, we may not ever fully understand God's reasonings or desires for us to do things, but when we come to know and better understand our relationship with Him, we can come to a place where we accept His will, and recognize His is better, so it is more desirable to walk as He desires and walk in His nature than it is to pursue our own.

Until we come to this place, we will forever struggle in our relationship with Him and our ability to be used by Him, for His purposes. There is freedom in relinquishing the need to have what we want all the time, because what God seeks and does through us is much better than earthly materialism and personal aspirations. God's service, within and through us, is never going to have the motivation of selfish purpose or gain. Whenever we are doing something with a purely selfish motive, we need to check ourselves to see if it's what God would have us to do…because it's probably not motivated by His prompting.

A Lesson from David's Life

If you've spent any time in church, you've probably heard about David. David was a King and Prophet in the Old Testament when the nation of Israel was a political entity trying to maintain its spiritual identity. In the long run, Israel lost its spiritual sense. Soon after, its political independence fell, as well. During David's reign, however, things seemed to stay together. There's several reasons why people think this is. They think he was good looking and strong in leadership, he was powerful over people, that he had prophetic insights, even the idea that he had a natural leadership ability. All these things may very well be the truth, but none of them explain the success of David's leadership. David was successful as a leader because he was, as the Scriptures call it, a "man after God's own heart."

"You did a foolish thing," Samuel told Saul. "You didn't follow the command of the Lord your God. If you had, the Lord would have established your kingdom over Israel permanently. But now your kingdom will not last. The Lord has searched for a man after His own heart. The Lord has appointed him as ruler of His people, because you didn't follow the command of the Lord." (1 Samuel 13:13-14)

Then the people demanded a king, so God gave them Saul, son of Kish, from the tribe of Benjamin. After forty years God removed Saul and made David their king. God spoke favorably about David. He said, "I have found that David, son of Jesse, is a man after my own heart. He will do everything I want him to do." (Acts 13:21-22)

I used to wonder why David was given the label, "a man after God's own heart." It didn't seem to me like David did things that were godly, at least some of the time. He lusted after Bathsheba and had her husband killed. His first child with her died due to his rebellion. He had trouble managing his own household. None of these things sound right, so how could David still be a man after God's own heart?

The problem wasn't with what the Bible says about David, it was with my concept of what it means to be a man after God's own heart. I was imposing my own ideas about that very issue onto the Scriptures and creating a conflict that wasn't there. The Bible never says a person after God's own heart must be sinless, perfect, flawless, and without human issues. Remember, the term is a man after God's own heart, not God Himself. It doesn't mean that David (or any of us) never miss the mark. What it does mean is that David had set himself on the leading – the guidance of God and the transformation of his heart – to follow the will of God for His life. David was selected to be king for this very reason. While Saul failed to remain faithful to God's precepts (even with the opportunity to repent), David kept God's desires in his sight.

The mark of perfection we often seek in Biblical characters (and ourselves) is found only in the life and work of Jesus Christ. Whenever we try to find it within us, we take our eyes off of Christ and His work, and looking for that in ourselves. When we do this, we have already ceased to have a heart God can use. Yes, we know the work Jesus has done for us is incredible, awesome, and life-changing, but it is also humbling. It reminds us of our own limitations and that our desire to do things the way we seek to do them, no matter what that "way" may be, are not the way of perfection, but ones of vanity. Our lives are a big ball of the good we do and the bad that we do, and our willingness to learn from all of it as we gain insight into the way we can be a man or a woman after God's own heart.

The good and the bad (sometimes the very bad) about David's life has been laid out for us to see to inspire our own faith and understanding as we grow and transform into individuals that God can use. David's life proves to us that it is a process to have a heart after God's own heart. We must go through the process of realizing ourselves, looking at our deeds and our overall lives for ourselves, getting honest with ourselves and who we are, being willing to listen to wise counsel, repenting, changing, and transforming into something more than we are right now. David was willing to do this in his process. No, he didn't do all things right, but he came to a point where he saw this clearly in his life and did what he needed to do in order to return back to God, to the path and understanding God had for Him, as he went along, failing, succeeding, repenting, seeking, and searching, sometimes in this order, sometimes in a different order, and sometimes in another order, still. David was willing to look at himself and hear what God had to say, and change accordingly, as necessary.

Where are you in this journey – do you have a heart God can use? Having a heart God can use is about the process, not perfection. The heart wants what it wants, and even the best of the best aren't always right or godly. The only way we break through ourselves is if we reach the point where we can say that it's God's will we desire, and that it is His will we desire to do. This means we deconstruct the things about us that keep us comfortable and secure and find that place where we are able to grow and gain insight into His understanding and purposeful place for us in this world.

(2)
GRACE-FULL AND SPIRIT-FILLED

How would you describe the Christian life? There are all sorts of ways people try to explain the manner of Christian living: holiness, purpose-driven, destined, meaningful, complete, spiritual. To a certain extent, all these terms are correct. Their vast differences (especially in connotation) display just how hard it is to try and explain the concept of being a believer. It's even harder to explain what it is like to be a person who is used by God in this world. The reason it is difficult is because when we talk about "use," we assume that being used or being usable means being abused. We don't want to make it sound demoralizing or demeaning, because that's not the God we serve. When we "use" something, we associate using it up or out and wearing things to a point where they can't be functional anymore. That's our human understanding of use; wearing out, abusing, misusing, and mistreating. Notice, though, that none of those words are "use." When we talk about being used by God, we are talking about our ability to operate as He would desire us to do so, so we can do His work and echo His purposes in this world. To do that, we must adopt a certain life posture that can be summarized in two ways: being grace-full and Spirit-filled.

When we talk about being "grace-full," I'm not talking about the elegant dance and gymnastic moves we see people do on television. I'll admit to not being the most graceful person in my movements. I'm short, I have balance issues, and for much of my life, when I walked, I'd stomp. It was all sorts of an issue for the adults around me, who kept telling me not to stomp and not be clumsy. That wasn't the best advice to give to a teenager, but they gave it anyway. They had a certain concept about how I should move and how I should present myself. I'd like to think they meant well. They were concerned about the way I would be perceived, because I wasn't very gentle in my presentation. In the church I grew up in, the way I was would never be acceptable. Truth be told, it's still not acceptable in many of the churches I was in as an adult. I didn't meet with their expectations of gracefulness, and that meant they felt I lacked something.

I did lack something; in fact, we had the same lack in common. None of us were "grace-full," or "full of grace." It wasn't something we thought we could be, because of our church doctrine. Being full of grace was reserved exclusively for Mary, the mother of Jesus. Those of us who were just regular people couldn't touch the concept for ourselves. We didn't learn it was possible for us to be grace-full, so it wasn't something we embodied.

We also had in common that none of us were "Spirit-filled." That wasn't a concept we even understood or considered, thus none of us embraced the idea of the Spirit of God living within us. The Spirit of God might have moved in our church leaders, in the general history of our denomination, but move in us – that was a different matter, all together. We considered ourselves churchgoing, identified ourselves by our denomination, were active within our local church and were participants of our belief systems, but none of us ever thought about the Spirit moving within us.

Over time, I have belonged to different denominations that have taught different things about our own reception of God's grace and of the principle of the Spirit's indwelling. Some churches emphasize God's grace working within us and exclude the Spirit's indwelling, and others emphasize the Spirit's indwelling, but exclude the grace of God. The truth is that we need both to be used by God, and we need both to survive as believers in this world (that often doesn't understand what we are about or what we are doing).

We can easily gloss these two issues over with exteriors that make us appear socially acceptable and "proper" to the church folk around us. The longer we are in church, the longer we learn how to model the things we see others do. We know how to dress, when to dance, when to shout, what posture to take during prayer, how to look the most "spiritual," how to walk into church with our big, huge Bible tucked within our arms, and what will make others respond best to us. It's not a big secret that we can look right, without really being right.

It's tempting to start thinking we are really right with God because we've found ways to camouflage. The proof is in the pudding, as they say. If we can't withstand the "life litmus test," seeing our faith in practical application, we aren't as right with God as we might think. If we are transformed, changed, new creatures, and growing in our faith, we should reflect that in how we live. When I say, "how we live," I don't mean that the long list of dos and don'ts that many churches use to measure individuals and their worthiness as believers. I'm talking about our ability to withstand the things we go through and go through them with the character and ability God desires we have. The Christian life, the Christian's relationship with God, can be summarized in one sentence: Learning how to love like God loves and learning to express that love as He would have us to do.

That's a mouthful; it's intended to be. God calls us to become more like Him, and less like our fallen selves that are all about self: selfish, self-absorbed, self-conceited, self-fulfilling, self-loving, and self-centered. The only way we do this is through grace and the Spirit. The only way it becomes increasingly possible is if we are full of both grace and the Spirit.

THE SECRET THINGS BELONG TO GOD

Pssst….you, reading this…come in…yeah, closer…I have a secret to tell you! Listen up, because it's a big one. You've probably never heard it before…are you ready? Yes? OK!

You are not a secret to God.

So maybe it's not the big secret you were hoping for, but it's an important realization to have in your life. Sometimes we get it in our minds that our church persona is who everyone – including God – believes we are. We can easily conclude that acting all "churchy" and that wonderful part we like to play to impress others is exactly who we are before God. It's true that God honors what we do for Him in honesty, but He doesn't honor when we are fake or pretending to be something we're not. That means every time you do something, and it sounds really good to others, but you do it with a wrong motive, God knows what's really inside of you and within you. Whatever you are really thinking, feeling, carrying around with you, your motives, how you live, how you feel, what you do, and the whys – all of that is bare before God.

Whoa. Let that set in.

I think there is part of us that doesn't really believe this. We hear so much about God knowing everything and then we hear about our sins being covered by the blood of Jesus. Part of us hopes that everything that's less than desirable gets swept under the blood, and God doesn't see it. Not so. Yes, God forgives our sins, our failings, our wrongdoings, but that doesn't mean God doesn't know what we do and is not aware of who we are.

Now, for the second part of the secret: God knows everything, and He loves us anyway.

This should be the bigger "whoa" than the first part, but it, unfortunately, is often the part of the message we roll our eyes at or nod at, somewhere, in the back of our minds, in silent disbelief or disagreement. I think that, as much as we don't really believe God knows everything about us, we also don't really believe God loves us, either. The love of God often feels distant and abstract because we can't see God, nor can we always feel His presence in the way we might wish we could. The spiritual realm doesn't always work like the natural does. We may want a human touch, a human feel, the presence of God in a tangible way...and we don't always get that. That doesn't mean God doesn't love us or care about us, but it means that we must adjust ourselves to the manifestations of the spiritual realm. Faith means we trust God for what we don't see, even when we may not feel Him or His presence in the way we might like. That's what makes faith hard, and what makes it difficult for people who don't believe in understanding. When we stand on faith, we receive what we may not feel, we may not always experience up close and personal, but we know, without a shadow of a doubt...it's there.

People look around when we talk about the love of God and ask, why is there suffering in the world? Why do children get cancer and die? Why are people starving? Why doesn't God solve all our problems? We could go over all these issues, point by point, and provide reasons as to why these things exist and why God doesn't just swoop down and erase all of them. The truth about our belief in God and our relationship with Him, however, is that we can't say we would love God more or believe in Him if He conformed to our image or ideal of what He should be. God loves us despite these different things we do, things that are against His will for us and His will for humanity. We love each other, at least most of us do, despite the things we do that are wrong...so why do we make the condition that we will only love God if He undoes what we do?

God knows us. He loves us despite what we do, who we are, even the ways that we don't love Him like we should. His love is evident in our salvation. When we receive that evidence, we receive Him. He loved us so much, the blood of Jesus, like we talked about earlier, is there to help us where we can't help ourselves. Yet our God, in His amazement, the same Being people debate about whether He exists or whether He really loves humanity, has still made a way to make sure His love for us is evident and manifest in a way we can understand and can empower us this side of heaven.

What can we say about all of this? If God is for us, who can be against us? God didn't spare His own Son but handed Him over to death for all of us. So He will also give us everything along with Him. Who will accuse those whom God has chosen? God has approved of them. Who will condemn them? Christ has died, and more importantly, He was brought back to life. Christ is in the honored position—the one next to God the Father on the heavenly throne. Christ also intercedes for us. What will separate us from the love Christ has for us? Can trouble, distress, persecution, hunger, nakedness, danger, or violent death separate us from His love? As Scripture says:

"We are being killed all day long because of you.
We are thought of as sheep to be slaughtered."

The One Who loves us gives us an overwhelming victory in all these difficulties. I am convinced that nothing can ever separate us from God's love which Christ Jesus our Lord shows us. We can't be separated by death or life, by angels or rulers, by anything in the present or anything in the future, by forces or powers in the world above or in the world below, or by anything else in creation. (Romans 8:31-39)

The evidence God loves us: Beyond Jesus (which is evidence enough), we find God's help to maintain our lives in a practical as well as spiritual way. He does this through grace, and through the gift (and manifestation through gifts) of the Spirit. It's unfortunate that we often don't understand either, but we don't understand them because we can't fathom them. Grace is more than just a nice idea; the Spirit is more than something to make us feel good in church. These two things help us realize the secret things that God knows and nobody else knows about…can be transformed.

New Creature, Old Issues

Many ask – and theologically debate – about the issue of sins committed after one becomes a believer. The obvious issue is that we still sin, even after we are saved. If we are really saved, are the sins we commit after salvation covered under Jesus' blood, or must we be forgiven all over again? If we are saved by faith, and we don't earn our salvation, what happens when we do sin after being saved? Does it mean we aren't really saved, or does it mean that sin doesn't matter once one becomes a believer? It's an interesting issue and an interesting debate, but it proves that we don't understand the work of grace from eternity past to eternity future for ourselves. We like grace as a musing, we like the idea of it, but when it comes to applying it for ourselves…well…we like the idea of doing things ourselves much, much better, and trying to make things work out, all on our own.

From the last chapter, we already discussed how much we like trying to make things work out, by our own means, on our own terms. Call it sadistic, call it masochistic, call it wrong, call it whatever you want to call it – it's what we like doing. The concept of saving ourselves isn't a task that tires us out as easily as we might like to think. We talk about being weary and exhausted from our works, but we keep them up, time and time again, because we get a certain sense pride from them. We love the idea that maybe this time will be the one where we get it right and everyone else gets it wrong. We might be saved, we might be a new creature in Christ, we might like to talk about old things passing away, but the truth is that we are a new creature with a lot of the same, old, boring issues that haven't died out so easily as we might hope they would. We become a new creature with the same flesh, the same us…the same egos, arrogance, judgments, tempers, temptations, flarings, bad attitudes, emotional fits, stubbornness, impatience, intolerance, and the like…and we must walk with God to figure out how to handle those things.

And that, my friends, is where grace enters the picture.

But God is rich in mercy because of His great love for us. We were dead because of our failures, but He made us alive together with Christ. (It is God's kindness that saved you.) God has brought us back to life together with Christ Jesus and has given us a position in heaven with Him. He did this through Christ Jesus out of His generosity to us in order to show His extremely rich kindness in the world to come. God saved you through faith as an act of kindness. You had nothing to do with it. Being saved is a gift from God. It's not the result of anything you've done, so no one can brag about it. God has made us what we are. He has created us in Christ Jesus to live lives filled with good works that He has prepared for us to do. (Ephesians 2:4-10)

The Bible teaches us that we are saved by grace through faith. It's not about being good enough, doing enough, having enough, or trying hard enough. It's a misnomer to say we are saved by faith alone, because faith is the catalyst by which saving grace comes into our lives in the first place. It's not faith alone that saves us; it's grace alone. Nothing but the grace of God can come, take this creature that wants to do everything the way it wants, and turn it into something other than where it started. It is truly God at work as He takes the best in us, redeems it, transforms it, and changes our perspective on just what it means to be "best" or "great." The best in us is there because of God – so He can polish, prime, and create within us a clean heart that is willing to serve Him.

We trip over grace because it's not just one thing. It's an entire expanse as God gives a part of Himself, His insights, and His love to us. Many translate grace as "unmerited favor," but grace is more than just favor we don't rightly deserve. God's Word translation of the Bible describes it as "kindness," but this still isn't a full picture of everything God gives us through His grace. It is a spiritual condition by which God gives us something freely, without question, when He doesn't have to. If we don't deserve it, then God doesn't have to give it to us, either. This means that grace is a statement of what God does for us and what we are given. It reveals something about both the Giver and the receiver. When we receive God's grace, it says something transforming about us, because we are receiving a part of God in our lives.

Even so then at this present time also there is a remnant according to the election of grace. And if by grace, then is it no more of works: otherwise grace is no more grace. But if it be of works, then it is no more grace: otherwise work is no more work. (Romans 11:5-6, KJV)

God gives us His grace, a part of Himself, because it's Who He is. God is love; love is transforming; it is saving; love gives; and love changes those who receive it. With God within our lives, within our very being, it changes us, from glory to glory and faith to faith, as we move away from that which is not love, that which we try to create for ourselves, on our own, in our own image.

Now our Lord Jesus Christ Himself, and God, even our Father, Which hath loved us, and hath given us everlasting consolation and good hope through grace, Comfort your hearts, and stablish you in every good word and work. (2 Thessalonians 2:16-17, KJV)

Grace is about salvation, but not exclusively in one context. Yes, grace is saving. It's amazing, and it is bigger than anything we can imagine. In our practical life application, grace is also something we experience every day, in many ways. Through grace, God saves us from ourselves. It's something we receive in our lives many times over and in many ways, even though the very act of salvation does not repeat. Grace permeates our existence and our experience, making God real at every pass and turn, even when it doesn't feel like it, and even when we aren't sure about what it all means. If we want to better understand about grace and its reception, we need to stand back and look at God, the Giver, ourselves, as the receivers, and see where God's grace is speaking to us in this life.

Grace is hard for us to receive and see working in our ordinary lives (at least at first) because it marks the end of doing things the way to which we are accustomed. If we truly receive grace in our lives, it means the transformation that comes about within us is truly from God. We are letting God work through us and within us, and it means we trust Him with every outcome, rather than trying to take over and orchestrate everything ourselves. In grace, we let go; we allow God to have His way; and we allow God to transform and touch our hearts, unlike anyone else.

...AND IT'S ALL OLD STUFF

We love walking in God's grace when we start to see it for what it is, but there's one thing about grace that's often not always easy to adjust to…it doesn't move very fast in us. Because the grace of God is there for what we need and to work within us, it moves at the pace of our spiritual walk…in other words, it works slowly. It is there for each situation that arises where we need that touch of God's intervention to bring us back to eternal reality.

I beseech you therefore, brethren, by the mercies of God, that ye present your bodies a living sacrifice, holy, acceptable unto God, which is your reasonable service. And be not conformed to this world: but be ye transformed by the renewing of your mind, that ye may prove what is that good, and acceptable, and perfect, will of God. For I say, through the grace given unto me, to every man that is among you, not to think of himself more highly than he ought to think; but to think soberly, according as God hath dealt to every man the measure of faith. (Romans 12:1-3, KJV)

In this world, we face incredible pressure to conform. We deal with the haunts of our lives and our pasts, things that have hurt us and forced us to stand out, and there is part of us that wants to bury our scars and look like everyone else. There is a myriad of ways we try to accomplish this goal; some seemingly healthy, some not so healthy, but all with the agenda to try and conform to something else, something that will make sure we don't stand out too much from the crowd. Who wants to be known by what they went through? Who wants to be remembered for the mistakes they made? Even worse, who wants to be judged?

"You are salt for the earth. But if salt loses its taste, how will it be made salty again? It is no longer good for anything except to be thrown out and trampled on by people.

You are light for the world. A city cannot be hidden when it is located on a hill. No one lights a lamp and puts it under a basket. Instead, everyone who lights a lamp puts it on a lamp stand. Then its light shines on everyone in the house. In the same way let your light shine in front of people. Then they will see the good that you do and praise your Father in heaven. (Matthew 5:13-16)

Imitate God, since you are the children He loves. Live in love as Christ also loved us. He gave his life for us as an offering and sacrifice, a soothing aroma to God.

Don't let sexual sin, perversion of any kind, or greed even be mentioned among you. This is not appropriate behavior for God's holy people. It's not right that dirty stories, foolish talk, or obscene jokes should be mentioned among you either. Instead, give thanks to God. (Ephesians 5:1-4)

We've learned the best way to get by is to fit in with others, but God doesn't desire us to fit in with everyone. We are called to be salt and light to the world. That means being noticed, because He has transformed us. He's taken all those things that we were ashamed of and turned them into a place of power, something that, while we might still be in process, we are coming a long way from where we were. It's by grace that this transformation can renew our minds, helping us align with the things of God that are good, acceptable, and perfect, showing us God's will in an understandable, rather than abstract, perspective.

God doesn't rush us along. Yes, there are times where we drag our feet and He tells us to pick them up and move along, but overall, the grace of God is there to help us as we deal with issues for the first time, the tenth time, or the thousandth time. I've had many a conversation with older or more seasoned believers who grow frustrated when they feel like an issue or problem that's from their past (sometimes their distant past) is front and center, as God taps on their shoulders about it again. Sometimes it's not the first time it's come up again. When they express to me how frustrating it is to have to go over things again or confront issues they feel they should be beyond, I point out that the concept that we are ever "done" in this walk with God is false. As long as we are breathing, as long as we are here, there will always be something for us to work through or work out. The ancients understood our spiritual walk to be cyclical rather than linear, thus meaning we will likely deal with things repeatedly over the course of a lifetime. The grace of God is there to help us on every step, and it's there to help us transform our minds. The work of salvation within us is a process, something we walk out with awe and amazement, and just like God, just like the perfection He is, we have just enough grace to walk out whatever we need to walk out.

So from now on we don't think of anyone from a human point of view. If we did think of Christ from a human point of view, we don't anymore. Whoever is a believer in Christ is a new creation. The old way of living has disappeared. A new way of living has come into existence. (2 Corinthians 5:16-17)

Everything we must walk out – it's all old stuff. They're all things that are a part of the old being, the part of us that surfaces so we can resolve it. All things are new for us, and that means we can approach them from a new point of view, a new way and a new perspective. Yes, it's all old stuff that pops up, but we aren't the same person. We don't have to deal with it the same way. Commit your way to the Lord and watch your progress in His grace.

GETTING FULL OF GRACE

You can never have too much grace. It's not like overeating on a holiday and then sitting in a corner, so stuffed you can't move. Grace has no calories, no weight with it, and no discomforts. It goes great with anything you wear, and it won't weigh you down. For this reason, it is our goal in life to get so full of grace, there is no room for old ways to take up space and reside within us.

It is God's desire that we can find a place of communion with Him that transcends a Sunday church service or an occasional Bible reading. It's amazing to think about all the things we do to fill our time and our space, to try and avoid those deeper talks and times with God. Grace, however, is a blessing that cuts through all the avoidance we carry when it comes to our relationship with God. Grace reminds us of the nature and character of God. He is good! Being full of His nature and character, and having it overflow within us and touch the lives of others is always, without a doubt, a great thing.

And of His fulness have all we received, and grace for grace. For the law was given by Moses, but grace and truth came by Jesus Christ. (John 1:16-17, KJV)

One of the promises for those who seek God in a deeper way is "grace for grace," or as some translations put it, "grace upon grace." Within the individual who seeks to receive and accept God's grace, we see the promise of grace upon grace upon grace, falling as layers and covering any area of life that needs God's favor and blessing. That's what it means to be full of grace; to allow God to move so fully within you that He overflows.

I said earlier that I don't think there is just one thing that describes grace. We often take different components of it and put it into one definition, excluding the others. The components of God's grace are:

- **Divine favor:** Favor indicates something is done or given out of the good intention, rather than because it is deserved or earned. Divine favor echoes the goodness of God, His incredible greatness to provide to us not what we always deserve or earn, but what reflects His good pleasure to give to us, His children.

- **Divine kindness:** Kindness indicates purpose, and is marked by ethics, which means it reflects the fairness of God as well as His concern for those of His creation.

- **Divine blessing:** Blessing is the bestowment of divine intervention in one's life. Whenever we are told to bless rather than curse, we are to impart and believe for the intervention of God's work in one's life, His free-flowing power and authority to move on someone's behalf.

- **Divine purpose:** Putting the other three components together, we find the concept of divine purpose. By such, we recognize life isn't a haphazard arrangement of events. While yes, sometimes things just happen because things happen, we know God is intentional about our lives. We can trust that, even though we don't always see the way, God has a purpose and plan for us in the bigger picture. Through grace, we tap into this purpose and discover more of His plan for us.

When we are full of grace, it means we are full of and receive God's divine favor, kindness, and blessing within ourselves. We take on these incredible things in exchange for the spirit of heaviness that often invades and permeates our lives. Like a lifting cloud, we are full of the grace of God, working to bring His purposes into full flow within our lives.

THE SPIRIT FILLS YOU

The work of the Holy Spirit is of frequent debate. There are two major theories about the work of the Holy Spirit. One states the Holy Spirit's activity has completely ceased and is no longer active today. The other states the Holy Spirit is still alive and active today, manifesting through various spiritual gifts and evidences in believers. Outside of these two points are dozens of subpoints, alternate ideas and concepts as to just how the Spirit works, moves, and impacts the lives of believers. In keeping with our concept of indwelling and overflow, to be usable by God, one must be "Spirit-filled."

The Scriptures teach us that God is a Spirit, and that we are to worship God in Spirit and in truth. This connects us to the work of the Holy Spirit, in a powerful way, within our worship and our relationship with God. Jesus promised us that when He returned to the Father, He would send us the Holy Spirit (sometimes called the Holy Ghost). We could define the Holy Spirit as "God in experience," because it is by the Holy Spirit that we experience the presence of God and see Him at work in our lives. Through the Holy Spirit, God provides us experience of Him, just as real and living today as it was in New Testament times.

Then Peter stood up with the eleven apostles. In a loud voice he said to them, "Men of Judea and everyone living in Jerusalem! You must understand this, so pay attention to what I say. These men are not drunk as you suppose. It's only nine in the morning. Rather, this is what the prophet Joel spoke about:

'In the last days, God says,
*   I will pour My Spirit on everyone.*
*   Your sons and daughters will speak what God has revealed.*
*   Your young men will see visions.*
*   Your old men will dream dreams.*
In those days
*   I will pour My Spirit on My servants, on both men and women.*
*   They will speak what God has revealed.*
*   I will work miracles in the sky and give signs on the earth:*

blood, fire, and clouds of smoke.
The sun will become dark,
and the moon will become as red as blood
before the terrifying day of the Lord comes.

Then whoever calls on the Name of the Lord will be saved.' (Acts 2:14-21)

This description proves the descent of the Holy Spirit is a part of prophecy, an echo back to something seen originally by an Old Testament prophet hundreds (or possibly thousands) of years before the first Christian Pentecost celebration. The disciples were given the ability to speak in the languages of heaven and heard by the diversity of people present, each understanding what was being said. There were numerous reasons why the Holy Spirit moved through the first disciples: to embolden them to proclaim the Gospel without fear, to live by the power of God in their lives, and to speak the Gospel, so it would be easily understood by the diverse crowd that was present there. This doesn't mean the work of the Spirit is restricted exclusively to the work of speaking in tongues (as it is commonly called), however. Wisdom or knowledge, the power to heal and be healed, the gift of faith, the gift of discerning spirits, the gift to work miracles, the gift to speak in prophecies or interpret prophecies, the gift of teaching, the gift of administration, the gift of mercy, the gift of helps, the gift of leadership, the gift of edification, the gift of giving, and of course not just the gift to speak in tongues, but to interpret tongues when the word given is for the body of the congregation are also spiritual gifts. The work of leadership within the church is spoken of as being a gift from the Holy Spirit. When we are Spirit-filled, the Spirit moves in any way that is necessary through us, and embodies the vision spoken of in Acts 2 to manifest unto purpose and gifting within the church today.

This is why it is so important to be Spirit-filled: the Spirit, as a living and active being, can impart just what is needed, how and when, to guide us into truth in every single circumstance and situation. We often talk about being led into all truth as if truth is exclusively something to know, to read on a page, but this is a misnomer. Truth is something that is lived and experienced, something we walk in, something we embrace and see firsthand, living and active. It doesn't change from age to age, but connects eternity with now, linking the past, the present, and the future. We must be Spirit-filled to have this encounter, this experience; to feel and know God is with us; and to embrace truth, recognizing it up close and personal at every point where its presence come to touch our lives.

The concept of being Spirit-filled (to parallel Pentecost) is to be so full of the Spirit, whatever comes out of you is of the Spirit, rather than of you. If we are truly Spirit-filled, we will not be able to hide our spiritual walk, even if it's not something that we readily talk about with others. They'll probably say there's just "something about you," or respond one of two ways: want to be around you or want to avoid you. That's the Spirit at work, comforting those who need it, convicting those who need to look at themselves, and bringing a general sense of truth to each situation.

BRINGING FORTH THE SPIRIT

In the Holy Bible in Modern English (translated by Ferrar Fenton), the translator describes Moses as being a "medium of the Holy Spirit." When I first read this, I took issue with the use of the term "medium" in connection with a Biblical prophet. When I thought more about it, the idea began to intrigue me for a whole new reason. The reason the translator used the term "medium" to describe Moses' relationship and purpose with the Holy Spirit was in contrast with those who were mediums of other spirits. What it says is that Moses allowed himself to be a literal conduit for the Holy Spirit, allowing the Spirit to overtake him and speak through him. It sounds weird, albeit a bit unorthodox, but it raises an important principle in our ability to be used by God and how the Spirit overtakes and works within us.

God's Spirit has made me. The breath of the Almighty gives me life. (Job 33:4)

The popular theory against Christians employing psychics and mediums is that utilizing such displays a lack of faith. This is surely a relevant point, but it is about far more than just a matter of trusting or not trusting in God. A psychic or a medium operates by a familiar spirit or a demonic spirit, which means they are full of something other than the Spirit of God. If we follow them, we aren't guided and directed by God. As believers, as people who want to make ourselves usable by God, we must always follow and embrace the work of the Spirit within us and within our lives. We can't chase after counterfeit spirits and adopt those as our guidance or within us and expect to be used by God.

The Spirit of God is always with us and always around us. We should never assume the Spirit of God comes in and goes out, and we should never, ever assume that something has an answer for us that is in no way connected to God. Yes, God does send prophets and individuals

38

into our lives that have spiritual gifts (such as prophecy, word of wisdom, and word of knowledge) to help us when we need a word or proper direction, but none of these gifts operate by a counterfeit spirit. The difference between a prophet, a prophetic gift or other spiritual gift, and a psychic is the spirit behind what is done and what is spoken. If we want to be used by God, we can't chase after things that are clearly not God and clearly prohibitive according to what He has revealed to us. Being used by God means embracing that Spirit, that Spirit Who is always around us and always working to transform and represent the experience of God within and through us, not catering to nor embracing counterfeit spirits.

This starts when we are honest with ourselves about our desires: our desire to know, in the immediate, and to look at things without wisdom. Whenever we start chasing after the unknown of this life, we forsake the eternal perspective we are supposed to be gaining.

But as Scripture says:

"No eye has seen,
    no ear has heard,
        and no mind has imagined
            the things that God has prepared
                for those who love Him."

God has revealed those things to us by His Spirit. The Spirit searches everything, especially the deep things of God. After all, who knows everything about a person except that person's own spirit? In the same way, no one has known everything about God except God's Spirit. Now, we didn't receive the spirit that belongs to the world. Instead, we received the Spirit Who comes from God so that we could know the things which God has freely given us. We don't speak about these things using teachings that are based on intellectual arguments like people do. Instead, we use the Spirit's teachings. We explain spiritual things to those who have the Spirit.

A person who isn't spiritual doesn't accept the teachings of God's Spirit. He thinks they're nonsense. He can't understand them because a person must be spiritual to evaluate them. Spiritual people evaluate everything but are subject to no one's evaluation.

"Who has known the mind of the Lord
    so that He can teach him?"

However, we have the mind of Christ. (1 Corinthians 2:9-16)

There will forever be a million reasons why the things that aren't of God and are not promptings of the Spirit will glitter as gold to get our attention. They look desirable because we do not view them with the mind of Christ. Sometimes we're impatient, sometimes we're tired, sometimes we're upset, and sometimes we're bored. These things are truly distractions, however, because the Spirit of God is always with us. Anything that draws us away from God and developing our experience with God is a distraction – and that means all these things that run around and operate by counterfeit spirits, offering us what we want in the right now rather than in the perspective of eternity – are distracting us from the Spirit's indwelling within our lives. It's still our choice to let the Spirit impact our lives and work in us unto the ultimate victory. We need to reach the point where doing right and becoming a part of that victory is about more than just getting what might be in it for us out of a situation. With the Spirit living in us, we are more than living in the here and now, with our issues, problems, and insecurities. A piece of the divine is within us, and we have part of eternity within us...so let the Spirit rule, and reign, as so desires, within our desires.

Fear

It might seem strange to talk about fear now, as we've been talking about being full of grace and full of God's Spirit. We understand the principle of being full of the things of God, but there are other things that often arise that block our ability to be full of all God desires us to be full of, to overflowing. The Scriptures list many spirits within its covers, but one of the most primary ones we hear about – and will likely encounter – is the spirit of fear.

Have you ever been afraid? Sure, we all have. Fear is something that comes upon us when we least expect it, and it easily intimidates us. There are people who find themselves afraid all the time, and then there are others who are afraid from time to time, but the fear never really goes away. It remains within us, rising at another point in time, reminding us of what we were afraid of before and how things didn't work right at an earlier point in time.

We call fear all sorts of things: a feeling, an emotion, a thought, a concept, an ideal, a sin, even a perception...but fear is identified as being a spirit. Because it's a spirit, that means it's not as simple as just wishing it away or hoping it will go away on its own. We can try to manage it, we try to handle our fears on our own, but because it's a spirit, fear isn't something we can just choose not to experience. What it does mean is that our spiritual perspective can greatly help in our handling of fear, especially when it rises within us.

When it comes to being grace-full and Spirit-filled, fear is something that stops and keeps us from learning and knowing God as we might desire. When we are afraid, we keep ourselves reserved, holding back, away from the truth about ourselves and about God. We keep ourselves from knowing Him fully and from discovering His will, thus meaning we flounder with discerning our own purpose.

There are probably a lot of things that I could say about fear. I could make an acronym out of it or go on a long diatribe about what it is and how it works, but we've all been afraid, and we all know what it does to us, within us. There are dozens of books available about fear, handling fear, how to be less afraid, and dealing with fear, but every one of us reaches a point where focusing so much on something (like fear) magnifies it more in our minds than not. When we are living with the spirit of fear as a controlling facet, it dominates our thoughts and ideas and makes us feel further and further away from the love of God. To be full of grace and full of the Spirit, we need to grab hold of the love of God in a way that strikes down fear and puts it in its proper place, which is not as the controlling facet of our lives.

Jesus told them, "It's Me. Don't be afraid!" (John 6:20)

So we can confidently say, "The Lord is my helper. I will not be afraid. What can mortals do to me?" (Hebrews 13:6)

God's love has reached its goal in us. So we look ahead with confidence to the day of judgment. While we are in this world, we are exactly like Him with regard to love. No fear exists where His love is. Rather, perfect love gets rid of fear, because fear involves punishment. The person who lives in fear doesn't have perfect love. (1 John 4:17-18)

There are many different Bible passages about fear and as pertain to the realms of fear and not needing to be afraid which are invoked repeatedly, but there's just one we need to resonate within us. All those things we are afraid of may be very real in light of the things we can see with our naked eye, such as bills, health, well-being, the future, disasters, or possibilities that may one day come (or not come, such as the situations may be), but they have one thing in common: when we are afraid, we are not looking to the love of God that has been completed and made available for us; we are looking to things that are temporal, passing away, that can change in an instant. When we exchange the eternal for the temporal, we will always experience fear in place of God's perfect love, which renders us the peace which passes all understanding.

It is only when we start to listen to the revelation of the Spirit of God, at work within us, to our infilling of the Spirit's presence, that we will stop listening to counterfeit spirits. The spirit of fear is not God revealing things to us that we need to know or be aware of, because it does not offer a solution. The love of God, which has been made complete, brings a completion; the Lord shows the issues, but He also guides to a solution, even if it comes in time.

We should not fear because God knows the end from the beginning. As our Creator, we have part with Him as He invites us to come into eternity with Him. When we live in His love, we will find fear ceases. This only comes about with time, as we walk in faith and trust Him to make eternity real and lasting for us. In the meantime, we take our walk step by step, and we allow the Spirit of God to indwell within us, pouring love within and casting fear out.

NO CONDEMNATION

Fear is something that exists here, not in eternity. Whenever we participate with fear, we worry about now rather than keep light of the eternal, bigger picture that God desires us to see full force. This is why fear is a spirit. It has a way of keeping us from God, creating distances and barriers between Him and us. One of the major reasons we experience fear, especially in connection with God, is because we fear the condemnation of God. Church has been great at establishing formalized systems that make sure we fear overstepping lines and boundaries that God often didn't invent, or maybe that are exaggerated versions of God's instruction. The Christian life is painted as an avoidance of things, of doing this, that, or something else, rather than moving toward God.

If you grew up in Sunday School (or spent any time in church as an adult), you probably heard about all the things God didn't want you to do. Drinking, smoking, dancing, playing cards, watching movies, listening to certain types of music, wearing certain types of clothing, engaging in sexual activity outside of marriage, and missing church were probably high up on the list of things you were not allowed to do. If you did any one of those things, you heard about God's extreme disappointment for you. You might have been made to repent at the altar or told that God was mad at you. You might not have heard much about loving God or God loving you, but you always heard about God and His anger, and it was reiterated that there was one thing that you didn't want to do…and that was make God angry.

Even now, sometimes the way we depict God makes it sound like being part of God's family is as dysfunctional as the ones in which we grew up. We don't talk about mature versions of our spirituality. Instead, we treat one another as children, not as individuals in a relationship with the Creator of all things. We are shamed and reprimanded, made to feel as if there is no hope for us and for every little thing we do wrong, God's going to get us.

These are old ideals and concepts based in the hope that we would learn how to do right through reinforcing punishment for our behavior. Our ancestors in the faith did the best they knew how to do by us. They believed things with all their hearts and lived their lives in a certain manner, with the belief that their values were right and were important. They fully believed there are consequences for our behavior. This is still true. There are consequences for what we do, and we must be prepared to understand consequences as a reality of life. The problem with over-emphasizing consequence and under-emphasizing the love of God and His grace in our life is that we start thinking all that awaits is consequence. I've met plenty of people who are so afraid of God they give up on pursuing relationship with Him. Others think they are going to be punished anyhow, so it doesn't matter if one is right with God and with doing the right thing, or not. When we present only one side of the message, we forget the essential nature of grace in our spiritual lives.

So those who are believers in Christ Jesus can no longer be condemned. The standards of the Spirit, who gives life through Christ Jesus, have set you free from the standards of sin and death. It is impossible to do what God's standards demand because of the weakness our human nature has. But God sent His Son to have a human nature as sinners have and to pay for sin. That way God condemned sin in our corrupt nature. Therefore, we, who do not live by our corrupt nature but by our spiritual nature, are able to meet God's standards in Moses' Teachings.

Those who live by the corrupt nature have the corrupt nature's attitude. But those who live by the spiritual nature have the spiritual nature's attitude. The corrupt nature's attitude leads to death. But the spiritual nature's attitude leads to life and peace. This is so because the corrupt nature has a hostile attitude toward God. It refuses to place itself under the authority of God's standards because it can't. Those who are under the control of the corrupt nature can't please God. But if God's Spirit lives in you, you are under the control of your spiritual nature, not your corrupt nature.

Whoever doesn't have the Spirit of Christ doesn't belong to Him. However, if Christ lives in you, your bodies are dead because of sin, but your spirits are alive because you have God's approval. Does the Spirit of the One Who brought Jesus back to life live in you? Then the One Who brought Christ back to life will also make your mortal bodies alive by His Spirit who lives in you.

So, brothers and sisters, we have no obligation to live the way our corrupt nature wants us to live. If you live by your corrupt nature, you are going to die. But if you use your spiritual nature to put to death the evil activities of the body, you will live. Certainly, all who are guided by God's Spirit are God's children. You haven't received the spirit of slaves that leads you into fear again. Instead, you have received the spirit of God's adopted children by which we call out, "Abba! Father!" The Spirit Himself testifies with our spirit that we are God's children. If we are His children, we are also God's heirs. If we share in Christ's suffering in order to share His glory, we are heirs together with Him. (Romans 8:1-17)

When we talk about there being "no condemnation" in Christ, it doesn't mean the wrong we do is without consequences. It does mean that our walk with God is not a long list of dos and don'ts. When the Spirit of Christ is on the inside of us, we learn to discern what is right and wrong as we listen to the Spirit's presence at work. It takes time to develop, and it helps when we have instruction in the Scriptures and good leaders and supporters who can help us better discern and understand the will of God in our lives. We must learn that we don't have to follow every impulse and desire that we might have. The sooner we gain insight into the concept that we don't have to sin or wrongdoing, the easier it becomes to walk away from destruction that often destroys and hurts us in the long run.

If we do something wrong, it's important to remember the old cliché, "We serve the God of second chances," isn't true. No, we serve a God Who offers us something better! We serve a God Who works with us as long as it takes to get it right. With every failing and fault, He is there to help us get back up again. In Christ, there is no condemnation, not because we will never sin again, but because as long as we keep working with God, He keeps picking us back up, helping us dust ourselves off, and try again. In God, when we are truly His, there is no end to His unfathomable love. It doesn't matter if it's the second time, or the fifth time, or the tenth time, or the two thousandth time. He's there, working with us, for as long as it takes.

<u>The Fruit of the Spirit</u>

How do we know if we have the Spirit at work within us? Many talk about the Spirit and talk about having it. Many believe the work of the Spirit is dependent on the number of gifts we have or the type of gifts we have. There are people who claim to have all the spiritual gifts, speak in tongues incessantly, operate in all the functions of the church, and work in all the helps ministries…but don't have any display of the Spirit in their lives. They might sing the loudest, run around the room first, and scream when they pray, but when it comes to really seeing the Spirit alive within them…there's nothing but dead-end, spiritual silence.

Surely there's no question that spiritual gifts are a sign of the Spirit's reality, but their purpose isn't to prove that we are full of the Spirit. Spiritual gifts exist to prove that the Spirit is real and active and at work in the church. We could say spiritual gifts are supposed to prove the church is full of the Spirit, not that individuals in the church are full of the Spirit. They prove that an individual is a part of the church, but not that the Spirit is indwelling in that person all the time. Spiritual gifts prove a person is periodically full of the Spirit, but not that the Spirit is guiding them on a regular basis.

Before anything else, the Spirit fills us to give us power. We are endowed with that power to live and move among this world, proclaiming the truth of the Gospel with everything from our lips to our every action. The power of the Spirit moves within us to change our lives. The more we allow His indwelling, the more we change.

There is a way to tell if a person is Spirit-filled regularly, and that is through the fruit of the Spirit. Galatians 5:22-23 tells us what the fruit of the Spirit is:

But the spiritual nature produces love, joy, peace, patience, kindness, goodness, faithfulness, gentleness, and self-control. There are no laws against things like that.

In Biblical times, people lived in agrarian societies dependent on agriculture. One's livelihood depended on productive crops, vines, and trees. The product of the work they did — their toil in the sun, temperament with the rain, and hopes for good soil — was the fruit, or product those crops brought forth. Whenever we start talking about fruit from a Biblical perspective, it's talking about the product of whatever work is going on within us. The more we pursue the work of the Spirit, the more we will display the product of the Spirit's work in our lives.

The fruit of the Spirit directly relates to our character and the way we interact with other people in our lives, as well as how we respond to God and our relationship with Him. When we display the fruit of the Spirit, we are telling the world that we are believers, living in God's goodness and grace, because of His unmerited favor and promise.

When we talk about being used by God, seldom do we talk on the fruit of the Spirit, which is a terrible shame. The fruit of the Spirit is the very character we need, summarized and put into a few memorable statements, to interact with others about God. One of the biggest complaints people have about Christians is that they are mean, unkind, stubborn, bull-headed, and insist that their way is right all the time. People frequently complain about not being able to talk to Christians, because Christians always must have the last word. This tells us two things about those who claim to represent the Christian way: First, they do not have a proper understanding of what God is about and what walking with God is about, and second, they aren't allowing themselves to be filled with the Spirit in their everyday lives. We can't "rah, rah, rah" the Spirit like we are some sort of cheerleaders during worship and then embrace messages that encourage us to be unkind, stubborn, and hateful toward others. No, we don't have to agree with everything everyone might do, but we do have to love others, even if they are different, even if they don't agree with us, and even if they never come around to the viewpoints many Christians claim to hold dear. If they were truly walking with the Spirit as they should, the fruit of the Spirit would result, which is the exact opposite of the issues many raise about believers today.

The fruit of the Spirit looks like:

- **Love:** *Love is patient. Love is kind. Love isn't jealous. It doesn't sing its own praises. It isn't arrogant. It isn't rude. It doesn't think about itself. It isn't irritable. It doesn't keep track of wrongs. It isn't happy when injustice is done, but it is happy with the truth. Love never stops being patient, never stops believing, never stops hoping, never gives up.* (1 Corinthians 13:4-7)

- **Joy:** *So I recommend the enjoyment of life. People have nothing better to do under the sun than to eat, drink, and enjoy themselves. This joy will stay with them while they work hard during their brief lives which God has given them under the sun.* (Ecclesiastes 8:15)

- **Peace:** *I'm leaving you peace. I'm giving you My peace. I don't give you the* *kind of peace that the world gives. So don't be troubled or cowardly.* (John 14:27)

- **Patience:** *For this reason we have not stopped praying for you since the day we heard about you. We ask God to fill you with the knowledge of His will through every kind of spiritual wisdom and insight. We ask this so that you will live the kind of lives that prove you belong to the Lord. Then you will want to please Him in every way as you grow in producing every kind of good work by this knowledge about God. We ask Him to strengthen you by His glorious might with all the power you need to patiently endure everything with joy.* (Colossians 1:9-11)

- **Kindness:** *But as long as I live, promise me that you will show me kindness because of the Lord. And even when I die, never stop being kind to my family. The Lord will wipe each of David's enemies off the face of the earth. At that time, if Jonathan's name is cut off from David's family, then may the Lord punish David's house." Once again Jonathan swore an oath to David because of his love for David. He loved David as much as he loved himself.* (1 Samuel 20:14-17)

- **Goodness:** *Let no man deceive you with vain words: for because of these things cometh the wrath of God upon the children of disobedience. Be not ye therefore partakers with them. For ye were sometimes darkness, but now are ye light in the Lord: walk as children of light: (For the fruit of the Spirit is in all goodness and righteousness and truth;) Proving what is acceptable unto the Lord.* (Ephesians 5:6-10, KJV)

- **Faithfulness:** *Beloved, it is a fine and faithful work that you are doing when you give any service to the [Christian] brethren, and [especially when they are] strangers. They have testified before the church of your love and friendship. You will do well to forward them on their journey [and you will please do so] in a way worthy of God's [service]. For these [traveling missionaries] have gone out for the Name's sake (for His sake) and are accepting nothing from the Gentiles (the heathen, the non-Israelites). So we ourselves ought to support such people [to welcome and provide for them], in order that we may be fellow workers in the Truth (the whole Gospel) and cooperate with its teachers.* (3 John 5-8, AMPC)

- **Gentleness:** *As holy people whom God has chosen and loved, be sympathetic, kind, humble, gentle, and patient. Put up with each other, and* *forgive each other if anyone has a complaint. Forgive as the Lord forgave you.* (Colossians 3:12-13)

- **Self-control:** *Because of this, make every effort to add integrity to your faith; and to integrity add knowledge; to knowledge add self-control; to self-control add endurance; to endurance add godliness; to godliness add Christian affection; and to Christian affection add love. If you have these qualities and they are increasing, it demonstrates that your knowledge about our Lord Jesus Christ is living and productive. If these qualities aren't present in your life, you're shortsighted and have forgotten that you were cleansed from your past sins. Therefore, brothers and sisters, use more effort to make God's calling and choosing of you secure.* (2 Peter 1:5-10)

These concepts are found throughout Scripture and are part of the nature we adapt as we gain deeper insights into the Spirit and in the will of God. As we fall in love with God even more, understanding His ways and seeing ourselves in eternity, we gain even more incredible insights and desire to let the Spirit move through us in a greater way. As we do so, our countenance should change. We should become more eager to love others, to walk in joy, to desire peace, to embody patience, to grow in kindness and goodness, to become more faithful and gentler, and to adopt greater self-control. The Spirit's work changes us, and we, in kind, change. The more the Spirit moves, the more usable and relatable we become.

A word on the fruit of the Spirit: the Bible makes it clear we cannot mock God. If we aren't really operating in His Spirit, desiring more of Him, or believing "for real," as many say, then God knows that. If we sow to the flesh, we will reap destruction; if we operate our work to mock God, we will reap destruction; but if we sow to the Spirit, we shall reap life. God knows the difference, whether everyone around you does, or not.

Make no mistake about this: You can never make a fool out of God. Whatever you plant is what you'll harvest. If you plant in the soil of your corrupt nature, you will harvest destruction. But if you plant in the soil of your spiritual nature, you will harvest everlasting life. (Galatians 6:7-8)

A LESSON FROM MARY'S LIFE

Mary, mother of Jesus, is not a mystery in the Scriptures. We don't know much of the details about her life, save the period when Jesus came into the world. We do also know she was a relevant and prominent figure in early New Testament history. Mary was the mother of Jesus, and this is important, but that's not the only reason why she was important. Mary was a person, a woman, who lived in an oppressive society and era of history. Despite the odds stacked against her, she became the first person ever who was both full of grace and Spirit-filled.

Six months after Elizabeth had become pregnant, God sent the angel Gabriel to Nazareth, a city in Galilee. The angel went to a virgin promised in marriage to a descendant of David named Joseph. The virgin's name was Mary.

When the angel entered her home, he greeted her and said, "You are favored by the Lord! The Lord is with you."

She was startled by what the angel said and tried to figure out what this greeting meant.

The angel told her,

"Don't be afraid, Mary. You have found favor with God.
You will become pregnant, give birth to a Son,
*   and name Him Jesus.*
He will be a great man
*   and will be called the Son of the Most High.*
The Lord God will give Him
*   the throne of His ancestor David.*
Your son will be king of Jacob's people forever,
*   and His kingdom will never end."*

Mary asked the angel, "How can this be? I'm a virgin."

The angel answered her, "The Holy Spirit will come to you, and the power of the Most High will overshadow you. Therefore, the holy child developing inside you will be called the Son of God.

"Elizabeth, your relative, is six months pregnant with a son in her old age. People said she couldn't have a child. But nothing is impossible for God."

Mary answered, "I am the Lord's servant. Let everything you've said happen to me."

Then the angel left her.

Soon afterward, Mary hurried to a city in the mountain region of Judah. She entered Zechariah's home and greeted Elizabeth.

When Elizabeth heard the greeting, she felt the baby kick. Elizabeth was filled with the Holy Spirit. She said in a loud voice, "You are the most blessed of all women, and blessed is the child that you will have. I feel blessed that the mother of my Lord is visiting me. As soon as I heard your greeting, I felt the baby jump for joy. You are blessed for believing that the Lord would keep His promise to you." (Luke 1:26-45)

When people talk about having incredible faith, I think of Mary. When I say I want God to move through me so I can believe for the impossible, I want to have Mary's faith. I want to believe so fully in our Lord that if He comes and tells me I will conceive by the power of the Spirit, without the assistance of my husband, I'll not only believe it's possible...I'll believe God will do it!

But it's important for us to remember that having that kind of faith isn't out of anyone's reach. Mary was just an ordinary person. She wasn't a celebrity, an internet star, or someone that anyone would have considered to be "important." She was someone who was living her life, making her plans, and expecting her life to follow a certain course of action. What Mary learned through her encounter with the Archangel Gabriel (and what we, in turn, should also learn), is something quite simple: Nothing is impossible with God.

Repeat that out loud: nothing is impossible with God. That thing you are dealing with can be overcome, because nothing is impossible with God. The issues you battle within yourself can be overcome, because nothing is impossible with God. The fear you experience can be alleviated, because nothing is impossible with God. If you are truly in Him and seeking Him for your life, nothing is impossible with God.

Why? Because with God, we have His grace, and we also have His Spirit. If the two are allowed to permeate and fill us, we will be able to look to God for everything and experience the fullness of life He has for us.

If Mary, who was a virgin, could conceive of the Holy Spirit and be full of grace for what was an incredibly impossible task (not possible by the order of nature, scientific interest, or any other logic or reason), then we can experience and be full of God's grace and Spirit-filled, as well. Our purpose for such is different, but the end goal is the same: we are endowed for our task, and our purpose in this world. The grace of God will carry us, and the Spirit of God will empower us. With these two, nothing will be impossible for us, because everything is possible within the will of God for us.

(3)
Doing Your Work

For we are God's [own] handiwork (His workmanship),
recreated in Christ Jesus, [born anew] that we may do
those good works which God predestined (planned beforehand) for us
[taking paths which He prepared ahead of time],
that we should walk in them [living the good life which He prearranged
and made ready for us to live].
(Ephesians 2:10, AMPC)

We've talked about what it means to have a heart that God can use and about the equipping for that process, and now we are to the fun part...the part where we have to do our work and get ourselves positioned for the things of God in our lives. Many times, we hear about doing the work of God as if getting full of grace, Spirit-filled, and usable by God is the end of the line, that God does everything, and we do nothing in the process. This is a misnomer, because God only works where He is welcome to work. If you do not desire to find His will and become a solid fixture within His plan of eternity, He will not force you. We all have things we need to encounter, deal with, overcome, and gain victory over to be truly usable by God, because there is a never-ending array of things that try to halt, stop, or hinder us along the way.

When we first decide we want to be usable for God, we are real into the process. It's new and exciting. We love the idea that we are going to do great things for God. We might not know exactly what He has for us to do, but the whole idea that we are going to do something that's part of a bigger, eternal plan takes us out of ourselves for awhile. The things that were once an issue aren't as much of a focus now, and we might easily think we have every problem licked. Then...life happens. Time goes by. Bills must be paid. Spouses are difficult to live with. Being single gets lonely. Kids get tiresome. Dogs must go out. Groceries must be bought. Work must get done. The things that were once an issue quickly catch up and find us, often with a vengeance. Sometimes it feels like we'll never, ever easily get out from it. The more the things we do become a priority, the more we push our callings, our promises, and the things we want to do long-term into the background.

We will forever find reasons not to do what God has called us to do. Believe it or not, it's not as hard to find reasons as you might think. The more up-close-and-personal the revelations are, the easier it becomes to find things to do to avoid discomfort or self-examination. The more we avoid this, the more obstinate and difficult we will easily become when we are confronted with ourselves. We won't like correction or discipline, and we will never want to look at ourselves and our role within our problematic situations.

To be usable by God, we must overcome ourselves, at least somewhat. We might not do it in totality, but we must get over those things which hinder us from obedience, those that keep us from developing proper spiritual awareness, listening to the voice of God, and gaining insight into things that happen in our lives from a spiritual perspective.

The ultimate goal of our spiritual lives is to see our natural lives in view of eternity, as a part of a bigger plan and purpose. This is how we become usable by God: we can identify our small selves in the midst of this much larger, cosmic plan, and see that as small as we might be, there is something for us to do. We don't all have the same calling, and we are not all called to do the same things. Discovering that purpose is often a good portion of the journey. Realizing how our gifts fit in the bigger picture, what we can do, and how we can contribute are amazing to see, but that's not where our purpose ends. We must apply ourselves, do our work, come to a place of understanding, and grow and mature enough to realize we can't do this without God. Everything in life will run out of excitement and thrill eventually, and all our problems will intensify and cycle until we are ready to change, but following the will of God gives us purpose and a place, something to hold onto and look forward to when we don't understand, and everything seems to fall apart.

As much as we've already worked on getting real with ourselves, now it's time to do the work that only every one of us can do.

DELIVERANCE FROM YOURSELF

I've often said that if there is only one thing we are delivered from in this life, it's ourselves. If you are never in need of a deliverance session, if you never have to get up and stand in that prayer line, if you never have to receive a word from someone else, if you never feel compelled to ask someone else for prayer, and if you are in such a state that you follow all the church rules to the letter of the law, you will still need to be delivered from yourself. Just because nobody else sees your weak moments and you don't feel they are there doesn't mean they aren't. Remember, God knows all, hears all, and sees all…so He knows who you are.

Deliverance from ourselves is hard – perhaps the hardest of all deliverances – because it is the only spiritual ailment that is completely socially acceptable. There are so many ways we idolize who we are and what we are doing…and nobody thinks twice about it because it's just the way we all think we're supposed to be. We're good at making everyone think we've got it all together and that we feel good about who we are, even if we don't and even if we shouldn't. The air of confidence is a part of our lives, a part of our success and survival, even if it's a complete and total lie or completely unmerited. We've learned to do what others do, imitate behavior, and venomously dislike or hate others because they don't reflect to us what we desire. As a result, we keep people around us who we like, who like us, who share our values…and we dislike challenge.

No matter how insulated and isolated you keep yourself, God is going to challenge you about who you are. It might not come all at once, but there will be many moments in your life when you see yourself through His eyes. It won't be the stellar, starlight view that you've had of yourself before this time. You won't enjoy it, but if you flow with it and follow God's leading, you will gain freedom from yourself and a step toward deliverance.

When I kept silent about my sins,
  my bones began to weaken because of my groaning all day long.
Day and night Your hand laid heavily on me.
My strength shriveled in the summer heat. Selah
  I made my sins known to You, and I did not cover up my guilt.
I decided to confess them to You, O Lord.
    Then You forgave all my sins. Selah
For this reason let all godly people pray to You
  when You may be found.
    Then raging floodwater will not reach them.
You are my hiding place.
You protect me from trouble.

You surround me with joyous songs of salvation. Selah
The Lord says,
   "I will instruct you.
   I will teach you the way that you should go.
   I will advise you as my eyes watch over you.
Don't be stubborn like a horse or mule.
   They need a bit and bridle in their mouth to restrain them,
      or they will not come near you."
Many heartaches await wicked people,
   but mercy surrounds those who trust the Lord.
Be glad and find joy in the Lord, you righteous people.
Sing with joy, all whose motives are decent. (Psalm 32:3-11)

Deliverance from oneself begins when we admit that we aren't perfect, all-sufficient, or right about everything. This gets sticky when it comes to the things of God. Our traditions (those things we discussed in an earlier chapter) have convinced us we are right about everything. We must be willing to admit we are wrong and have done wrong, and what we are wrong and have done wrong, for God to use us. Why is this important? If we are going to be used by God, we must be taught by Him.

Yes, it's awesome to have great spiritual leaders. If you have a great leader who you know God speaks through, then keep them. Listen to them and embrace what they have to say to you. The reality, however, is that your leader is not available seven days a week, 24 hours a day. You are going to have moments where it's just you and God, dealing with a situation or a matter, and you must be able to hear from God as to what to do and how to do it. At some point in time, you may outgrow where you are, as well as your leadership, and need directions on what's next and what to look for next. Having great leaders doesn't nullify our need to be taught of God for ourselves, although the level that we might learn from God might be different than a leader or someone with teaching authority. We still must answer to God and stand before Him and learn what He desires to show us for ourselves. It might not be information or education that is for anyone but us, but God reveals Himself to us as He teaches us. If we want to know God, we must be teachable.

A teachable spirit starts when we are willing to get over ourselves and let God work through us. Our resistance to His influence and movement within our lives is at the very heart of the pride and arrogance from which we must be delivered. If we have it with God, we surely have it in other places as well. The only way we can come clean with it is through God's gracious guidance and instruction.

(Dis)Honesty

We've already talked about honesty and about the ways we describe our true monetary desires with altruistic-sounding concerns and feelings. Now we are going to address honesty with ourselves and with others in a more general, "doing your work" kind of sense. If we lie about our true feelings as relate to money, we lie about other things, too. If we are honest with ourselves (as we are attempting to do here), most of us lie all the time, without a second thought about it.

Why is lying so common? The truth costs us something. It costs us a part of ourselves and our comforts, our worldview and our concepts of ourselves. We don't tell the truth because the truth costs us too much, and we lie because it's easy. It's that simple, and that complicated.

One of my side jobs (aside from ministry) is publishing. I have spent over twenty years in editing, and I frequently edit for individuals who are not always full-service clients (as well as those who are). Over the years, I've come across more than a few individuals who submit manuscripts for editing and are emphatic about "how good the book is." They tell me that others in their lives thought they were so noteworthy and had so many things to say, they should write a book – and lo and behold, here is the book. They are also quick to say how many of those same people read either part or all of their manuscripts and think the book is great. When I look at the book, I sit there and shake my head in total disbelief. Odds are good, if someone comes to me and starts off by telling me how great the book is, it's probably not that great of a book. In these situations, the book is usually a grammatical nightmare, the thoughts are not cohesive, and the writing quality is quite poor. Because everyone around them told them the book was great, I am now in a position to either rewrite the book for them or let them publish a book that's a mess (with some grammatical and editorial changes, of course) that's really just not very good. You can't tell me that with some of these books, people read them and really thought they were that great. That can only mean one thing: people lied to them. Why did they lie? Because lying was easy. It was easier than being honest, telling them the truth about the quality of their work. In the process, they let people pursue a lie, thinking they are good at something they aren't, and refusing to be honest about real strengths and very real weaknesses.

I call this approach "foundational dishonesty" because our foundation with ourselves and others is inherently dishonest. We don't admit we dropped the ball on a project or didn't do the right thing, we say we were "too busy," or we turn the situation on our leaders and those we are accountable to and make them out to be the bad guys. We get angry and defensive when we are wrong and avoid telling others the truths that stare them – and us – right in the face. We lie to ourselves, we lie to other people, we lie at church, and we even try to lie to God. God knows better, but it doesn't change the fact that we stand before the Almighty and try to talk our way out of things we shouldn't have done. At the core of our being, we are encouraged to be dishonest and handle things with dishonesty and outright deceit.

There are six things that the Lord hates,
even seven that are disgusting to Him:
arrogant eyes,
a lying tongue,
hands that kill innocent people,
a mind devising wicked plans,
feet that are quick to do wrong,
a dishonest witness spitting out lies,
and a person who spreads conflict among relatives. (Proverbs 6:16-20)

I picked this verse for one reason: this verse lists five different things that relate to dishonesty that the Lord hates (a lying tongue, a mind devising wickedness, feet that do wrong, a dishonest, lying witness, and someone who spreads conflict). It doesn't just say it's something that's a little bit bad before God, but indicates they are hateful to God, things that can't stand in His presence. We like to point and mock specific issues or feel that the Bible pits sins against each other, but dishonesty is at the absolute top of God's list of things that we should not do…and so often, we do it, without even a thought.

Never steal, lie, or deceive your neighbor. (Leviticus 19:11)

In honesty, ask God to show you yourself, and where you are living dishonestly or falsely. Ask God to show you where you are dishonest with yourself and with others. Instead of taking the easy way out with all those lies and untruths, speak truth. You don't have to speak it rudely or unseemly but speak what is true. Speak reality, not clouded-over fluff. Make a point to be direct with people. Accentuate what is true, embracing and loving truth in your life, because it is truly what has the power to set you free. In other words: stop lying.

ACCOUNTABILITY

We hear a lot about accountability today, as a comfortable buzzword that's usually shouted from the pulpit or on social media by frustrated leaders who don't feel they are seeing enough "accountability" in the people they lead. There can be any number of reasons for this, but one of the things I've come to notice is that while we might talk about accountability, it's not something that we teach on often enough or with enough clarity for people to truly understand what we are talking about.

When accountability arises in a situation, a leader usually uses the term to indicate a person, or a group of people aren't quick to step up and admit when they've done something wrong. There's a great deal of pressure on people to act accordingly, and when they don't, things tend to go awry.

A few years ago, however, God showed me that accountability is more than just admitting when we've done something wrong or fessing up to things. Accountability starts long before problems arise, and it's usually in the form of recognizing our place in community. Through accountability, we accept what we do well and being responsible for that. This means accountability starts with honesty – when we are honest with ourselves and when others are honest with us about our strong points and our weaknesses. We receive what is spoken in genuine love and honesty for our edification and stop thinking everyone else is out to get us or just hate us because we aren't like them (and we will discuss this more, later). The essence of accountability is being willing to be responsible for the whole of our being, for the whole of ourselves.

There are all sorts of ways people have tried to instill accountability within the church today, but many of those ways have faltered. Yes, having great leaders is important, but it's not everything. If we don't set ourselves to apply God's principles in our lives, our leaders can't help us become what God wants us to be. Accountability partners were a trend for awhile, as two or more people set themselves up to be "accountable:" contact each other when things arise and to pray for one another. Accountability partners are fine to a certain extent, but the truth is that we need to learn how to stand on our own before God. That's what every leader, every person in authority, and yes, even every accountability partner should prepare you to handle. We should not ever see accountability as something exclusive, as something only reserved for our leaders or for our accountability partners, but as something that relates to the entire body of Christ. If we are called to be a part of that body and we are called to bring forth our abilities, our purposes, and our very selves for that service, then we need to be willing to be accountable for that to the entire body. It doesn't mean we answer to everyone all the time, but that we are willing to be responsible, to own our calling and our purpose, before the entire body of Christ.

As you know, the human body is not made up of only one part, but of many parts. Suppose a foot says, "I'm not a hand, so I'm not part of the body!" Would that mean it's no longer part of the body? Or suppose an ear says, "I'm not an eye, so I'm not a part of the body!" Would that mean it's no longer part of the body? If the whole body were an eye, how could it hear? If the whole body were an ear, how could it smell? So God put each and every part of the body together as he wanted it. How could it be a body if it only had one part? So there are many parts but one body.

An eye can't say to a hand, "I don't need you!" Or again, the head can't say to the feet, "I don't need you!" The opposite is true. The parts of the body that we think are weaker are the ones we really need. The parts of the body that we think are less honorable are the ones we give special honor. So our unpresentable parts are made more presentable. However, our presentable parts don't need this kind of treatment. God has put the body together and given special honor to the part that doesn't have it. God's purpose was that the body should not be divided but rather that all of its parts should feel the same concern for each other. If one part of the body suffers, all the other parts share its suffering. If one part is praised, all the others share in its happiness. (1 Corinthians 12:14-26)

Whether you are called to serve in a leadership position of ministry or not (and most people are not, so if that's not you, you're not alone), you are called to offer what God has given you to the continued function and purpose of the church. It takes all of us, being accountable, making ourselves aware, standing up for what we do, admitting what we don't do, and being who we are, walking out the servanthood of our call, to do this thing called "church."

OH, THOSE HATERS!

I recently saw a TikTok reel by which an exasperated preacher made the point that much of the modern church thinks its issues are due to either the devil or haters. He aptly pointed out they don't read their Bible, pray, tithe, attend church regularly, or devote themselves to the ways of God, but they still believe the reason they have no power in their lives is because of Satan and haters. In a few words, he eloquently established their problems aren't haters, or Satan, or anyone else. If that's how you're living, then your problems are very clearly...you.

We can't ever (or maybe it's we won't ever) be accountable if we think everyone is "hating" on us all the time. Sit back sometime and watch the amount of "hater" accusations you'll find on social media. We love to talk about people tearing us down and being negative when they point out our faults or that we aren't doing something properly, but is it fair to deem that as always being "negative?" Sure, there are some people who have nothing good to say, ever, but is it really a matter that anyone who points out anything about us that we don't want to hear is "hating" us? We aren't always good at, or able to do the things we desire to do in this life, and let's be honest – someone must have the dirty, uncomfortable job of setting the record straight in our lives. No, it's not for everyone to do and not everyone who does it does it with the right motives, but not everyone who brings us to a place of confrontation does so out of "hating."

When I was young, I had red, curly, kinky hair that I could never do anything with. I hated having that hair. It was ugly and difficult to tame and it just...wasn't the statement I wanted to make. I wanted long, straight, black hair like my friend had. She was of Brazilian and Italian ancestry, and her skin was a creamy, olive color that meant she tanned easily. I wanted to be able to tan and have dark hair like my friend had instead of red hair and the whitest skin anyone in my family had ever seen (which I later learned, much later, at that, was due to albinism).

My mother told me that I was never going to be tan, that I needed to take care of my skin and wear sunscreen. When my sister dyed her hair black and looked awful, my mother made it really clear that I could do whatever I wanted to do to my hair, but it would look as awful as hers did. (So, she didn't get that right – I've come to love this dyed, dark hair!) When I got a sunburn (sometimes through my own fault, sometimes not), that sunburn had to be treated. It would come up again, every time – I had to take care of my skin. Sunburns aren't a joke. I was never going to be tan, I was never going to have long, black hair (unless it came out of a bottle). Like it or not, this is what I got.

Now how ridiculous would it sound if I called my mom a "hater" for telling me that and deliberately went right back out to burn? I don't even think my mom hated me for saying I'd look bad with black hair (none of us knew how good it would look until I tried it). However, if I deliberately pursued such things without a sensible thought, you would call me foolish, not my mom a "hater." Why? My mom told me the truth; she told me a fact about myself that I needed to accept to move forward with my life and to keep from getting very sick. I needed to be accountable for myself and accept the fact that I was never, ever, going to get a tan in my life and do something else, instead.

You can say this is different – you can say this is not the same – you can say that your situation doesn't sound like this – but some of us are just as absurd with the things people tell us about ourselves that we refuse to receive. We are that little albino kid out on the soccer field with a third-degree sunburn because we refused to wear sunscreen. We're going to show up everybody else and do it our way, even though our way is both wrong and unreasonable. We don't want to deal with what others tell us because we don't like it. We don't like having to confront that who we think we are and what we think we are good at aren't realities.

As Jesus was saying this, many people believed in Him. So Jesus said to those Jews who believed in Him, "If you live by what I say, you are truly My disciples. You will know the truth, and the truth will set you free."

They replied to Jesus, "We are Abraham's descendants, and we've never been anyone's slaves. So how can You say that we will be set free?"

Jesus answered them, "I can guarantee this truth: Whoever lives a sinful life is a slave to sin. A slave doesn't live in the home forever, but a son does. So if the Son sets you free, you will be absolutely free. I know that you're Abraham's descendants. However, you want to kill Me because you don't like what I'm saying. What I'm saying is what I have seen in My Father's presence. But you do what you've heard from your father."

The Jews replied to Jesus, "Abraham is our father."

Jesus told them, "If you were Abraham's children, you would do what Abraham did. I am a man Who has told you the truth that I heard from God. But now you want to kill Me. Abraham wouldn't have done that. You're doing what your father does."

The Jews said to Jesus, "We're not illegitimate children. God is our only Father."

Jesus told them, "If God were your Father, you would love Me. After all, I'm here, and I came from God. I didn't come on My own. Instead, God sent Me. Why don't you understand the language I use? Is it because you can't understand the words I use? You come from your father, the devil, and you desire to do what your father wants you to do. The devil was a murderer from the beginning. He has never been truthful. He doesn't know what the truth is. Whenever he tells a lie, he's doing what comes naturally to him. He's a liar and the father of lies. So you don't believe Me because I tell the truth. Can any of you convict Me of committing a sin? If I'm telling the truth, why don't you believe Me? The person who belongs to God understands what God says. You don't understand because you don't belong to God." (John 8:30-47)

Jesus' words to these people were not what they wanted to hear. They were neither positive words, nor uplifting. It wasn't words that made them feel comfortable or comforted. They were hard truths that those people needed to hear: who they thought they were was simply not who they really were. If nobody ever told them the truth about their situation, they would never get on the right track to change. Speaking these truths, however, didn't make Jesus a "hater." He wasn't speaking to them out of hate; He was speaking to them out of truth.

This doesn't mean any of us have the right to go around and speak to people any which way we want. Jesus wasn't speaking out of an angry, fleshly tirade when He spoke to people. A truth spoken out of the flesh is still of the flesh, and that makes it easily wrong and quickly offensive. We are to speak what's true in love, directly and honestly, without aiming to do so out of our own flesh or our own frustrations. We are only able to do this if we hear Jesus speaking to each one of us in this passage, that we need to come to accept the truth of ourselves, stop looking so intently at the truth of other people, and accept that in all things, we may not be the faithful, bouncy people we believe ourselves to be. We all deal with sin, we deal with believing things that just aren't true some of the time, and we uphold traditions so we can remain comfortable in ourselves. If we hear Jesus calling us out of comfort (illegitimacy) and into truth (legitimacy), we will find it a lot easier to receive the truth about ourselves and better able to speak in love to others.

Yes, there are people who are jealous of our abilities and successes and don't want to see us succeed. Yes, there are people who see our potential and don't want us to develop it. However, this is not every single person who points out a flaw in you, or every single situation where you don't get feedback for something you might hope to receive. There's reality and there is accountability, and reality and accountability demand we are real with ourselves about what we can really do. Not everyone in the world is created to write a book, preach a sermon, teach a class, start a church, be on television, preach all over the world, or have what is deemed as a "high" office of ministry. I'd say most people are not called to do these things. Most people are called to be good at and embrace their other abilities in a multitude of ways, doing things that benefit and bless the lives of their families, friends, congregations, and others around them, everyday. There's nothing wrong with this; it's just different from what some others are called to do. This doesn't mean anyone hates us if they point out realities; it simply means we are here to embrace the truth and grow in our own sense of accountability from every situation that causes us to stretch and mature within our purpose.

PASSING FROM GUILT TO PURPOSE

If there's one thing most of us learned from growing up in a general sense of life, it is guilt. Two of the earliest disciplinary methods many parents use are shame and embarrassment, causing us to feel bad for things that we did (or sometimes things we didn't even do). Guilt's purpose was to make us aware of what we did and make sure when we did something wrong, we felt bad about it. We could say it was an "aversion" therapy to wrongdoing: we would feel so bad about what we did, we wouldn't do it anymore.

There are two flip sides to guilt, especially in the context I just spoke about. I understand the reason our parents, guardians, and those entrusted to our care used guilt as a tool to try and keep us away from wrong or from redoing something we shouldn't have done. Using guilt for this purpose was designed to attach the feeling of guilt to our wrongdoing and thus keep us from avoiding it in the future. Our elders hoped we would associate wrongdoing with feeling bad, which is an entirely reasonable premise. The problem is that we would have gaps in our "bad feelings" because we reached a point where getting away with doing something bad often felt pretty good. It would give its own natural high, so we would avoid feeling bad for what we did. Guilt had, and still has, a funny way of popping up where it desires. Some things that we do wrong we feel nothing about, and others plague us for years. There are those who feel guilty all the time, about everything, even things that have nothing to do with them, or are long over. Then, there are those who are so selectively guilty, it doesn't seem anything phases them.

Both of those positions represent extremes. What we will look at here is something in between the two: guilt that pops up here and there, selectively, and the purpose it is, or isn't serving in any given situation. See, over the years, we've grown accustomed to the feeling of guilt. It doesn't sting as much now as it often once did. As the pace our lives move is much, much faster than it was when we were young, we don't always respond to guilt in the same way we once did. Something might come up and we might feel bad for a little while about it, but we don't do anything to correct it. This is also often conditioning from youth; while someone might have made sure we felt bad, they didn't always have the ability to make sure we righted situations. Now, as adults, we've learned how to feel guilty, but we don't turn that guilt into momentum to fix a situation.

When I was going through a trying transitional time in my ministry, I dealt with the frustration of having outgrown most of the people who were closest to this work. At one time, they were trusted people whose thoughts and perspectives helped me to make decisions. The longer time went by, I saw their advice falter and questioned much of their loyalty. When I raised issues, such as lack of support and involvement or financial giving, I would get apologies. They would feel bad; they felt guilty for not doing what they were supposed to do. Yet as time went by, they wouldn't do anything to make the situation right. Their uncomfortable feelings would either pass into a return to normal or they would grow distant into oblivion.

The thing I would always say is what I am going to say here, in this book: I am not going to tell anyone not to feel guilty, unless the guilt has reached a point that is unreasonable or isn't suitable within a situation. I don't think it's advisable we get totally out of touch with guilt and create barriers and walls to make sure we don't ever feel guilty. Even in situations where we feel guilty without warrant, we need to learn how to appropriately experience guilt rather than saying we should just never feel guilty again. Guilt is our indicator that we haven't done something right. If you feel bad about something, you need to let that move you to make a situation right and do what you are supposed to do, because I can't work with you feeling bad. Feeling bad is just that – a feeling – and that feeling can easily change or wane with time. I've learned over many years of ministry that while guilt might pop up to make us aware of things, it isn't something that is going to help us maintain our lives and do the right thing as a long-term plan.

I made my sins known to You, and I did not cover up my guilt.
I decided to confess them to You, O Lord.
  Then You forgave all my sins. Selah (Psalm 32:5)

Now my bitter experience turns into peace.
  You have saved me and kept me from the rotting pit.
    You have thrown all my sins behind You. (Isaiah 38:17)

God is faithful and reliable. If we confess our sins, He forgives them and cleanses us from everything we've done wrong. (1 John 1:9)

When we experience guilt, our response should be repentance rather than waiting for the feelings associated with guilt to pass. We should go before God, allow Him to transform us, forgive us, and show us the way to that which is right. What is more important for us to do is pass from guilt to purpose and admit where our priorities really are and why we don't do the right thing when we don't do it. Instead of wasting time on guilt, we need to spend time on action. If our season is up somewhere or we are pursuing too many things or things we ought not to pursue, we need to admit and acknowledge that rather than feeling guilty because we are always dropping the ball. (That expression, "dropping the ball," is, a nice way of saying that we didn't do the right thing.)

If we walk in purpose, we will be far less tempted to function in guilt cycles that go nowhere and lead to nothing but long-term avoidance of where we need to be. What is our purpose? How do we discover this? How do we make ourselves of most service to God, allowing Him to move through us? How do we tighten the reigns on our lives to make sure that we aren't inviting guilt to enter the picture and dominate us?

DISCOVERING YOUR PURPOSE

Discovering your purpose begins when you become self-aware. When I speak on being "self-aware," I don't mean you become self-centered or that your entire world is you. Far from it! Being self-aware means being aware of your position in the world, in the church, and conscientious of your strengths and weaknesses. In being self-aware, we know ourselves well enough to know what we should pursue and what we shouldn't.

Figuring out purpose can be tricky, especially in the light of the fact that everyday life often doesn't seem very purposeful or meaningful. Sometimes pursuits become about anything and everything that's available to us, and it's easy to get caught up, lost, or sidestep in the insanity of everyday life. There are days when we step back and wonder, what if this is all there is? The same issues, struggles, and problems, for years on end – what if this is the end of the line?

Perhaps the most important thing we can do in the discovery of purpose is divorce ourselves from the idea that everything we do, see, and experience right now is all there is. It's tempting to think our jobs are how we're supposed to spend the rest of our lives, our situations at home won't ever improve, and that what we see is forever what we get.

Problem is, we are missing God in this picture. In our haste to change – often change we think we want until we have it – we forget the idea that God is just as much God right now as He is after a circumstance changes. If we don't recognize God in our right now, menial as it sometimes feels, we are missing the principle of eternity present in everything we do.

The indwelling of the Spirit within us is to give us the perspective of eternity, seeing things through God's perspective so we will understand His will. Our everyday lives are our training ground, a place where we are stretched to develop the fruit of the Spirit in our lives in a far deeper way. The same God Who stretched out the heavenlies is the same God Who inspired all the different aspects of everyday life: cleaning, neatness, attention to everyday details, self-discipline, productive work, cooking, structure, family life, childcare, friends, and enjoyment of life. This means there is a connection between the things we do and the things that we do for eternity. As the Spirit works and moves within us, we are better able to see what we are supposed to learn through the moments of impact and growth in our lives.

Most people, even famous people or people who the world deems as "important" still must do ordinary things and do them well. We all have errands to run, people to meet, other people to interact and live with, jobs to do, and lives to lead, often that don't feel very glamorous or important, at least some of the time. It's in those times that we can order ourselves properly, act in a godly manner, and conduct ourselves with an eternal vision.

Certainly, all who are guided by God's Spirit are God's children. (Romans 8:14)

Where can I go to get away from Your Spirit?
Where can I run to get away from You?
  If I go up to heaven, You are there.
  If I make my bed in hell, You are there.
  If I climb upward on the rays of the morning sun
    or land on the most distant shore of the sea where the sun sets,
      even there Your hand would guide me
        and Your right hand would hold on to me.
  If I say, "Let the darkness hide me
  and let the light around me turn into night,"
    even the darkness is not too dark for You.
      Night is as bright as day.
      Darkness and light are the same to You. (Psalm 139:7-12)

If there is nowhere we can get away from God, it is the Spirit of God that reminds us of His constant presence in our lives. That means when we cut someone off in the mall parking lot, when we flip someone the middle finger in traffic, when we yell at someone else in an angry outburst over nothing, when we just don't do what we've committed to do, and all those other things that are less than stellar, the Spirit of God reminds us that God is there. He bids for us to examine why we react in the way we do. That same Spirit is also there when we don't feel very purposeful, reminding us of the bigger, more eternal, picture. What we are doing right now is only for this moment; the moment will pass, and it will no longer be here again.

Our purpose is different than our calling in that our underlying purpose is to know God in all things, to worship and love Him, and to know Him for ourselves. It sounds tricky when we start breaking it down by things, but ultimately, we all have the same purpose. How we find it may vary slightly depending on our calling, but our purpose is to know, love, and serve God. It doesn't matter if we are called to be a missionary in a foreign land, a preacher here at home, an honest businessman or businesswoman, a professional or tradesperson, or even someone who cleans a home or an office. No matter what that calling is, it will lead you to a greater sense of God's purpose in your life.

LOVING LIKE GOD REQUIRES

In doing our work, our long-term purpose is to love others as God would ask us, to love as God does. In reading the Scriptures, it's easy to gloss over the nice, sweet verses that talk about love, whether it's loving enemies or friends. They sound good to us, but we don't often apply them in quite the way we should. If we are to be honest, we spend a lot of time trying to find ways to avoid loving our neighbor. We twist our judgments and say we really talk out of our nasty flesh because we love people, but we know we are just trying to find ways not to really delve into the love of God. In the Song of Solomon 8:6, we read a very powerful, very expressive passage on love and the descriptiveness of its nature:

Wear me as a signet ring on your heart,
as a ring on your hand.
Love is as overpowering as death.
Devotion is as unyielding as the grave.
Love's flames are flames of fire,
flames that come from the Lord.

These are words we need to consider in the concept of loving our neighbor, loving our enemies, and even loving everyone, because they express the intense desire with which God loves us. See, in Bible times, God was able to reveal something through Scripture's words that are applicable for all times: people are really good at loving when it comes easy, but don't love quite so well when it's more difficult. The concept of loving someone who loves you or reflects on you is easy. It gets more difficult when they don't look like you or if they don't like or love you back, for whatever reason. God commands us to stand, just as He does, loving humanity through their good and their bad, expressing the truth and relevance of that love, even when we don't get it back. We are called to be consistent in love in an inconsistent world, offering others – even if they have no use for us – something eternal.

If we love others, we will make a point to be all the things we discuss in the fruit of the Spirit: loving, joyful, peaceful, patient, kind, good, faithful, humble, and self-controlling. Now ask yourself: do I love like God requires?

When I look around, I am amazed to see how few people can truly get along with others. I hear almost daily about someone cutting someone off, not speaking to someone anymore, feeling slighted by someone (often with justification), and general discord among families, friends, churches, communities, and nations. People want to pray the general prayer for "marriages," for an institution and for the continuation of an institution, but they do not pray for the individual people who are in a marriage. People want to pray the general prayer for "families," for an institution and the continuation of that institution, but not the people who face issues, day in and day out, that we cannot fathom and don't bother to help with. We sit and argue, quarreling over this political issue or that one, trying to convince people that our perspective is the most moral, most accurate, most correct, and we never stop to look at ourselves. We are so caught up in issues and being heard, getting people to understand where we are coming from and feeling like our needs in the debate are met, we have reduced our entire world perspective to a one-sided political issue and the need to make sure everyone knows we are "right" about it.

…And don't we all love to be right?! (That's the wrong love to have, by the way!)

Our need to be fed is causing us to lose the world because we don't love anyone. We can say we love God, but does the church right now really love God? Do we, who claim to be part of the church, love God enough to know Him, to read the Scriptures, to engage with Him, to spend time in His presence, or is He just a musing that we use to forge battles with others and create useless debates and wars that have no purpose? Are we using God to try and further ourselves, our own attempts to cling and hold on to the past? Are we using God as an excuse to avoid our own issues, and point the finger at everyone else? Have we made God another politic…and is that just maybe why we aren't transforming the world?

The Scriptures tell us that judgment starts in the house of God, but it doesn't say how God does it. As I sit back and watch the church's reaction to multiple modern issues, I am noting that God is using the world to judge us. We are quick to balk at the way other religions operate, but the second they are treated and regarded by the world in a way that we feel Christians are not treated, we throw a royal fit. Whether we want to deal with it or not, Christianity is held to a higher standard than other religious groups. The reason for this is our own doing: we are the ones who have set the bar high, who talk about love and understanding and wanting people to come to know a God Who is love. We clearly want love to work for us when we want to win the argument or things to swing in our favor, but love is there for those times when we don't win the argument, and things don't go in our favor. God is waiting for us to measure up to this Book, this doctrine in which we claim to believe, right up beyond where it gets uncomfortable for us. The only way that we are judged is if we are put into situations where we must confront ourselves. In this, God is pressuring us, through the world. He is judging us and expects us to measure up.

Our behaviors are simply not in alignment with the love that God requires us to have. The way we act, sometimes spoken of in love, is not what Jesus told us to do. If we are not living and loving as God requires, we will not exemplify the character we are supposed to have.

If we are to truly live in love, we must realize that love is about laying ourselves down. All of ourselves: our opinions, feelings, the need to be right, all of it, to love someone else in pursuit of the Gospel. When we take on the title of "Christian," Christ is to be our identity. When we love-but-not-love others, we tell them, "I'll love you, but I won't love what you do…" or "I'll love the sinner but hate the sin…" we are automatically making sure they know how we feel about any particular topic at hand. We have set ourselves to make judgments and establish right and wrong, but seldom, if ever, do we do it out of a true sense of God's love. Instead of trying to establish our points, which reflect how much we love ourselves, why don't we just tell others we love them? Why does everyone need to know, all the time, where you stand on everything? Being so overly opinionated blocks the Spirit's opportunity to flow through you...and we all know that is something we truly do not want to do. Let love say something so powerful, so transforming, something that says, "I am willing to lay down how I feel about any issue and stand as a witness to that before you," that you can allow yourself to be His vessel.

I may speak in the languages of humans and of angels. But if I don't have love, I am a loud gong or a clashing cymbal. I may have the gift to speak what God has revealed, and I may understand all mysteries and have all knowledge. I may even have enough faith to move mountains. But if I don't have love, I am nothing. I may even give away all that I have and give up my body to be burned. But if I don't have love, none of these things will help me.

Love is patient. Love is kind. Love isn't jealous. It doesn't sing its own praises. It isn't arrogant. It isn't rude. It doesn't think about itself. It isn't irritable. It doesn't keep track of wrongs. It isn't happy when injustice is done, but it is happy with the truth. Love never stops being patient, never stops believing, never stops hoping, never gives up.

Love never comes to an end. There is the gift of speaking what God has revealed, but it will no longer be used. There is the gift of speaking in other languages, but it will stop by itself. There is the gift of knowledge, but it will no longer be used. Our knowledge is incomplete and our ability to speak what God has revealed is incomplete. But when what is complete comes, then what is incomplete will no longer be used. When I was a child, I spoke like a child, thought like a child, and reasoned like a child. When I became an adult, I no longer used childish ways. Now we see a blurred image in a mirror. Then we will see very clearly. Now my knowledge is incomplete. Then I will have complete knowledge as God has complete knowledge of me.

So these three things remain: faith, hope, and love. But the best one of these is love. (1 Corinthians 13:1-13)

We've all read the chapter on love in 1 Corinthians 13 so many times, we skim over just what it says. We know it says something relevant, but our inability to examine it properly means we skim over the important parts. We all love reiterating that love is patient and kind and that it doesn't keep a record of wrongs, but if we think about how we interact with others in general, it's pretty safe to say the love we are supposed to have is not in us. I believe one of the most tell-tale verses in 1 Corinthians 13 is also one of them we almost never touch on, and that is found in verse 5:

- *Love...it doesn't think about itself...*
- *Love... (God's love in us) does not insist on its own rights or its own way for it is not self-seeking...* (AMPC)
- *Charity... seeketh not her own...* (KJV)
- *Love... isn't always "me first"...*(MSG)

In love, we are not all about ourselves. That is what God requires. It's easy to follow false teaching that makes the Kingdom all about us and what we can get out of it; but this isn't what God asks of us. Love doesn't seek its own way! To avoid the judgment of God, we must adopt a proper walk of love and love like God loves, learning the true principles of intimacy, sustained upon love and honor through their lives. We must stop only loving as is easy...because if it is all about what is easiest for us, it's not really love.

<u>A LESSON FROM THE APOSTLE PAUL'S LIFE</u>

The Apostle Paul was a central figure in the early years of Christianity. He represented its change from a loosely knit group of individuals who had all had an experience that changed their lives to a growing, thriving body of believers in multiple locations. His writings reveal to us so much of what was going on at that point in history, both in a general sense and the immediate sense of the church. His writings, even controversial to this day in many circles, mark the change and passing of the church from a limited experience to a universal one, with all the complications and difficulties that came along with that change.

The change seen in the writings of Paul is not just of those of the church's experience. The Apostle Paul's words also reflect a change within him, going from where he started out to where he wound up. I think when we read his words, we often take for granted his own personal spiritual process as it is contained within them. Paul wasn't any better than we are, and that can be seen in many of his words. He dealt with frustration, temper, loneliness, poor health, and the ultimate difficulty of becoming all God wanted him to be. Because we don't look at him in this light, as a person with struggles to attain greater insights and spiritual depths, we often forget about his own spiritual transformation.

"I'm a Jew. I was born and raised in the city of Tarsus in Cilicia and received my education from Gamaliel here in Jerusalem. My education was in the strict laws

handed down by our ancestors. I was as devoted to God as all of you are today. I persecuted people who followed the way of Christ: I tied up men and women and put them into prison until they were executed. The chief priest and the entire council of our leaders can prove that I did this. In fact, they even gave me letters to take to the Jewish community in the city of Damascus. I was going there to tie up believers and bring them back to Jerusalem to punish them.

"But as I was on my way and approaching the city of Damascus about noon, a bright light from heaven suddenly flashed around me. I fell to the ground and heard a voice asking me, 'Saul! Saul! Why are you persecuting Me?'

"I answered, 'Who are you, sir?'

"The person told me, 'I'm Jesus from Nazareth, the One you're persecuting.'

"The men who were with me saw the light but didn't understand what the person who was speaking to Me said.

"Then I asked, 'What do you want me to do, Lord?'

"The Lord told me, 'Get up! Go into the city of Damascus, and you'll be told everything I've arranged for you to do.'

"I was blind because the light had been so bright. So the men who were with me led me into the city of Damascus.

"A man named Ananias lived in Damascus. He was a devout person who followed Moses' Teachings. All the Jews living in Damascus spoke highly of him. He came to me, stood beside me, and said, 'Brother Saul, receive your sight!' At that moment my sight came back and I could see Ananias.

"Ananias said, 'The God of our ancestors has chosen you to know His will, to see the One Who has God's approval, and to hear Him speak to you. You will be His witness and will tell everyone what you have seen and heard. What are you waiting for now? Get up! Be baptized, and have your sins washed away as you call on His Name.'

"After that, I returned to Jerusalem. While I was praying in the temple courtyard, I fell into a trance and saw the Lord. He told me, 'Hurry! Get out of Jerusalem immediately. The people here won't accept your testimony about Me.'

"I said, 'Lord, people here know that I went from synagogue to synagogue to imprison and whip those who believe in You. When Stephen, who witnessed about you, was being killed, I was standing there. I approved of his death and guarded the coats of those who were murdering him.'

"But the Lord told me, 'Go! I'll send you on a mission. You'll go far away to people who aren't Jewish.'" (Acts 22:3-21)

The Apostle Paul was a man who was willing to do his work, for decades, as he loved and served God. Before his conversion, Saul was the ultimate "alpha male." He thought he knew it all and was never afraid to use his brawn to intimidate and threaten others. He had people killed because he had the power and authority to do so. Now, we fast-forward to his epistles, and we find a man who speaks about developing the characteristics of love, humility, gentleness, and operating as a Spirit-led individual, one who sought to use the impact of God upon people rather than all his brawn and brains.

Paul didn't just fall off a horse one day after a spiritual encounter and became all the things he spoke of needing to be in the Scriptures. There's a 15-year span between Paul's conversion and his ministry as an apostle. Over those years, Paul worked on his life and transformation to serve as an apostle, which also changed him more as time continued.

So then, as Christians, do you have any encouragement? Do you have any comfort from love? Do you have any spiritual relationships? Do you have any sympathy and compassion? Then fill me with joy by having the same attitude and the same love, living in harmony, and keeping one purpose in mind. Don't act out of selfish ambition or be conceited. Instead, humbly think of others as being better than yourselves. Don't be concerned only about your own interests, but also be concerned about the interests of others. Have the same attitude that Christ Jesus had.

Although He was in the form of God and equal with God,
*   He did not take advantage of this equality.*
Instead, He emptied Himself by taking on the form of a servant,
*   by becoming like other humans,*
*   by having a human appearance.*
He humbled Himself by becoming obedient to the point of death,
*   death on a cross.*
This is why God has given Him an exceptional honor—
*   the Name honored above all other names—*
*   so that at the Name of Jesus everyone in heaven, on earth,*

and in the world below will kneel
and confess that Jesus Christ is Lord
to the glory of God the Father.

My dear friends, you have always obeyed, not only when I was with you but even more now that I'm absent. In the same way continue to work out your salvation with fear and trembling. It is God Who produces in you the desires and actions that please Him.

Do everything without complaining or arguing. Then you will be blameless and innocent. You will be God's children without any faults among people who are crooked and corrupt. You will shine like stars among them in the world as you hold firmly to the word of life. Then I can brag on the day of Christ that my effort was not wasted and that my work produced results. My life is being poured out as a part of the sacrifice and service I offer to God for your faith. Yet, I am filled with joy, and I share that joy with all of you. For this same reason you also should be filled with joy and share that joy with me. (Philippians 2:1-18)

The Apostle Paul's ministry had the influence it did, down to the present day, because he was willing to do his work – confront himself and become something other than he was by his immediate nature. He followed Christ's example of humility, emptying himself of whatever rights he might have felt he had, and walked in a position of humility, obeying God and working the salvation of God within himself. His advice – to avoid complaining and arguing, remaining blameless and innocent, reminds us all that joy comes as we are willing to do our work, be responsible for ourselves, and love others. We will never find what we seek if we are unwilling to do the work of emptying ourselves so God can fill us up with things much better – His grace and His Spirit.

(4)
PRAYING YOUR WAY THROUGH

Let my prayer be accepted as sweet-smelling incense in Your presence.
Let the lifting up of my hands in prayer be accepted
as an evening sacrifice.
(Psalm 141:2)

I once heard it said that the rays from the sun, as they descend over the clouds, are actually the prayers of God's people rising to heaven. This may not be scientifically sound, but it is nonetheless a beautiful image of prayers going before God. It's beautiful because it's a visual for us of the true beauty in prayer, marking prayer as something as beautiful before God as the rays of the sun against the clouds. It's unfortunate that we don't often think of prayer as a beautiful thing, but it is something that transforms us, and our perspective on our relationship with God in a radical way.

When we don't understand the important connection between communication and relationship, we don't understand the value in prayer. When I decided to write about prayer for the first time, many years ago, I immediately remembered being young and in traditional church settings. The church I attended as a child engaged in prayer in the same way it had since around the sixteenth century. Prayers were read by the priest, who read them from a book, and then the congregation would respond with a tired "amen" as soon as he finished speaking. Prayers were always formal, and never spontaneous. We were never taught about praying from the heart or praying out of what we desired to say or speak to God. It's not that such was really forbidden, but it just wasn't something that was ever on the table. One of the cornerstones of our religious education was learning the church's textbook prayers, those that were spoken for centuries and a central part of our faith formation. It seemed as if there was one of these scripted prayers for everything, every event under the sun. There were prayers for things we lost, when we were having trouble with our families, when we had hopeless cases, for specific jobs or situations in our lives, literally everything. We had patron saints, individuals to whom we prayed in these specific situations. A prayer consisting of many words and several implications had been penned and printed on small cards or small pocket-sized books for every need. We were told how we could pray, how we should pray, the posture we should adopt for prayer, when we should pray, and even what we should pray about. Every aspect of our prayer lives was penned and detailed by someone else, either living or dead, who may or may not have had the slightest idea of what we were going through and what we were facing in our modern times. Prayer wasn't really seen or taught as a communication with God, but rather, a scripted rehearsal of lines pre-prepared to, hopefully, gain attention and favor with those who were deemed most able to grant what we needed.

When I became a Christian, I had no idea how to pray or what prayer really was. I thought prayer was this big, formal event scripted by a book. In looking to other Christians around me, I didn't find much help in learning the correct paths to prayer. Others around me were poor models of proper prayer due to their own religious backgrounds. Most people I met in those early years had a similarly uncomfortable and awkward approach to prayer. It was as if our prayer lives were completely stumped without a book in front of us to define what a prayer was. They might have tried to pray in public and master spontaneous prayer, but most repeated themselves multiple times, over and over again, with what they could think of to say, quickly and offhand.

It's probably safe to say many people are confused about prayer in one way or another. At the very least, they are extremely intimidated by prayer and the process it takes. Whether it's misunderstanding what prayer is itself or misunderstanding how to pray, most have problems with prayer to the point where it trips them up or negatively impacts their prayer lives. Not surprisingly, they do not receive satisfaction in their prayer lives or with the answers God sends to them.

If you want to be used by God, you must know how to pray.

CREATED FOR RELATIONSHIP

One of the most common questions I am asked by those who are either not sure what they believe or are not Christian in their understanding is, "Why be a Christian? What makes Christianity special?" The question is usually asked in earnest. It is my opinion that it's a fair question to ask. Christianity is not the only belief system in the world. If you live in most western nations, it's not even the only belief system in the city where you live or maybe in your neighborhood. We live in a day and age where we don't often attend the church our parents attended because we don't feel a mandatory generational identification with a belief system for ourselves anymore. Whether this is good or bad isn't the point; it's a reality. We have choices and options now, and with those choices and options comes the responsibility to choose accordingly for what we seek. It also means the church must step up its game and answer these questions in a relevant manner, not putting others down or treating anyone as if they are diminished for their questions or thoughts.

The answer to the question that I give, however, is not real complicated. It's practical: God creates us for relationship, and within our understanding in Christianity, it is the only belief system where God has reached out to humanity to bridge the communication gap that existed, not just between Him and us, but between all of us, one to another. Rather than expecting us to reach out and randomly offer just to Him, He made the way for us. This is unlike any other deity or figure in any of the major world religions, and that is something we need to take note of and respond favorably in reaction. It doesn't mean we never have questions (it's fine to have questions) and it doesn't mean we always understand everything (we don't always understand everything), but the faith of Christianity, manifest thanks to the person and work of Christ, gives us something other religious experiences cannot. That is true relationship, something where we can receive and give, something that fills us so we can give it out again, and something that can change the very fabric of who we are, for the better.

Look at it this way: At the right time, while we were still helpless, Christ died for ungodly people. Finding someone who would die for a godly person is rare. Maybe someone would have the courage to die for a good person. Christ died for us while we were still sinners. This demonstrates God's love for us.

Since Christ's blood has now given us God's approval, we are even more certain that Christ will save us from God's anger. If the death of His Son restored our relationship with God while we were still His enemies, we are even more certain that, because of this restored relationship, the life of His Son will save us. In addition, our Lord Jesus Christ lets us continue to brag about God. After all, it is through Christ that we now have this restored relationship with God. (Romans 5:6-11)

God created us for relationship. Jesus' major purpose, through His life, His teachings, His ministry, His death, and His resurrection, was relationship. Our purpose in church, brought near from far off into the family of God, is relationship. Everything we do in this life is about relationship; not just any kind of relationship, but spiritually sound and healthy relationships.

If we are created for relationship, prayer is a part of that relationship. We pray for ourselves, we pray just to talk to God, we pray for others, and we pray for situations of all sorts, from the small to the large. Prayer is a part of our relationship with God as a central cornerstone of it, but it's not just about our relationship with God. As we pray, we grow in our understandings of matters, we grow spiritually, we develop new insights and change, and we pray for others. The whole of prayer, and of its relevance, relates to relationship.

If we adopt a prayer life that is entirely scripted (as many do) we overlook the principle of relationship that is just about life: life right now, the future, our thoughts, feelings, hopes, dreams, destiny, and all the things we can't easily script about life. While there's nothing wrong with enjoying the prayers that others have written throughout the centuries and praying them, there is something wrong if that's all we pray. Approaching prayer in this way leaves gaps, because it doesn't represent the heart of the person right now, and it doesn't represent the needs of that relationship.

Prayer reminds us that for a relationship to be solid, there must be communication. Yes, God has reached out to us, but we must reach out in response to what He has done and do our part. Prayer isn't just about a long list of us doing the talking and voicing what we expect God to do; it is about having a relationship with the Almighty that changes us and changes our perspectives on everything. When we view prayer like this, we should all be the first to desire to run straight to our place of prayer, on a regular basis, to foster our foundational relationship with God and others.

CREATED TO COMMUNICATE

When people talk about relationships (especially marriages) today, there are many complaints about the issues frequently present. Any assortment of self-help books and so-called experts will assign marital troubles and issues to different things: lack of money, not enough sex, stress, having to work many long hours, disagreements, disunity, unspoken hostilities, and unfulfilled dreams. The baseline of most, if not all issues in a marriage, however, often relate to lack of communication. We didn't grow up in a world that fostered or encouraged healthy communication, so we often attribute relationship issues to any number of peripheral issues that have communication as their root. Couples don't fight about money, they fight about power; they don't fight about sex, they fight about intimacy; they don't fight about stress and working, they fight about not being able to rely on each other; they don't fight over unfulfilled dreams, they fight over dissatisfaction. We've been taught to be indirect rather than state what's really behind our surface matters. That means we've learned how to fight over subjects rather than communicate real issues.

…And we do fight over subjects. The mere suggestion we should be more honest about our feelings sends us into a state of shock. After all, we're giving the laundry list of things that bother us…so what's the problem? The problem is that we often don't have the language to communicate our true feelings. We fight over subjects, not realizing what's really behind them. We don't want to face the truth about our relationships because we don't want to face the truth of ourselves.

Then we wonder why we have a hard time with prayer.

One of the reasons we are uncomfortable with prayer is because prayer is direct rather than indirect. When it's just us with God or a group of us praying with God, we are uncertain as to how to be direct and clear in our communication. We think it's easier to stick to subjects, rather than communicating the essence of something to the Almighty. Because we haven't been taught to communicate well, we are often uncomfortable when we are in situations that require direct communication. The very thing people often try to market as prayer to those who aren't real familiar with it – it's a direct communication with God – is the very thing that can make people uncomfortable with it, especially if they aren't exactly sure where they stand in their faith.

Once Jesus was praying in a certain place. When He stopped praying, one of His disciples said to Him, "Lord, teach us to pray as John taught his disciples." (Luke 11:1)

It's fascinating to me that when it came to understanding prayer, the disciples came to Jesus because they observed His prayer life. They were able to see, from His ability to talk to masses, that He was a communicator and knew how to communicate to the Father. The request was that they desired to be taught how to pray, not necessarily always what to pray. They were asking Jesus to help them be better communicators in prayer, more effective and clearer, because they realized their prayer skills could be better. They knew they couldn't have a good relationship with their Creator if they didn't communicate with Him. That the One to ask is the One Who came forth from the Creator, as part of Him.

It's obvious from this singular verse that communication has been hard for people for centuries. Learning to be clear and effective in prayer is something that is tricky for many. It also means there must have been some general confusion about prayer, even back then. The Scriptures give us indication of common religious methods of prayer employed in the first century. Many of them are still in use today: pray long, pray wordy, and pray very publicly.

"When you pray, don't be like hypocrites. They like to stand in synagogues and on street corners to pray so that everyone can see them. I can guarantee this truth: That will be their only reward. When you pray, go to your room and close the door. Pray privately to your Father Who is with you. Your Father sees what you do in private. He will reward you.

"When you pray, don't ramble like heathens who think they'll be heard if they talk a lot. Don't be like them. Your Father knows what you need before you ask Him. (Matthew 6:5-8)

Jesus spoke on these matters as He did because they do not indicate, nor assist, with relationship. Prayer was seen as a display of spiritual splendor, not communication with God. This is the very reason why we need to be taught how to pray: we need to know how to communicate. When we are children, we learn how to speak by uttering sounds and repeating the words we hear around us. As we approach prayer, we need to learn how to speak rightly, from the heart, and not use prayer as a way to imitate what the supposedly super-spiritual people around us do. We must adjust our ideas of prayer, our concepts of it, and speak directly to God in our private, personal time with Him. It doesn't mean we can't pray in public or as part of a worship service, but we must spend devotional time with the Father, void of distractions, displays, and exterior ideals that will take the relationship out of prayer.

Another key to effective prayer is to limit word usage. We have no need to make a big display of our prayers, nor do we have to talk on and on excessively, because God knows our needs. We are in a relationship with God; that means God knows us and knows our needs, before we even voice them. When praying, we ask God in faith, knowing He will provide us with an answer. Littering prayer with many words doesn't make it more effective, powerful, elegant, or purposeful…it just makes it long. Prayer isn't a speech we make; it's not a monologue.

When we pray, if it's not about using a lot of words, what should we pray? Jesus answers this in Matthew 6:9-15:

"This is how you should pray:
Our Father in heaven,
*   let Your Name be kept holy.*
*   Let Your Kingdom come.*
*   Let Your will be done on earth*
*   as it is done in heaven.*
*   Give us our daily bread today.*
*   Forgive us as we forgive others.*
*   Don't allow us to be tempted.*
*   Instead, rescue us from the evil one.*

"If you forgive the failures of others, your heavenly Father will also forgive you. But if you don't forgive others, your Father will not forgive your failures."

Jesus makes prayer easy for us here, as a foundational communication. He outlines a few major areas for us to cover in our prayers. If we examine – and practice – these areas, we can be assured an effective and joyful prayer life. They are:

- Praise the Name of God
- Pray for Kingdom matters
- Pray for necessities
- Pray for forgiveness
- Pray against temptations
- Pray for all that belongs to God

PRAISE THE NAME OF GOD

In Biblical times, a person's name represented something about themselves and their family lineage. It represented all a person was, with the full of their reputation (good or bad) and where they came from. This is why the Bible speaks so much about the Name of God and the Name of Jesus; the Name represented all that God is and all that God desired to do. When we speak, honor, or hallow His Name, we are honoring the entirety of all that Name represents.

To praise the Name of God is to echo and herald all that He is, even that which is beyond our comprehension and beyond what we can effectively state in descriptive terms. In Old Testament times, the Name of God was considered so hallowed (holy, sacred), scholars and teachers believed sinful people (thus, everybody) shouldn't even speak the Name of God out of their mouths, because to do so would be to profane it. This is how serious believers regarded God's Name. It was not a cuss word, a profanity, something to be spoken carelessly, or something to be spoken without proper understanding of all the power associated with it. It was, in its essence, everything that represented the power, majesty, and grandeur of our God.

Today, we don't know exactly (with a hundred percent certainty) just what the Name of God is or how it should be pronounced. Efforts to keep from speaking the Name of God led its use to go out of vernacular. Even though there are a number of groups who claim to know the "true" Name of God and state you must use their version to be saved, this isn't true. None of us know just what the Name of God is. This doesn't mean, however, that we can't hallow the Name of God. We might not be able to hallow it literally from our lips, but we can do a few things instead.

The first is we can honor God any time we see a divine title or variation on the divine Name. Whether Yahweh, Jehovah, Lord God, Lord of Hosts, or some other variation, we can respect that such is a reference to our God, and honor that. Secondly, we can call on God through these different methods. God knows Who He is, and He knows when we call upon Him. Whether we address Him as Abba, Father, Lord, Savior, God, Almighty, or any other way that we honor Who He is. Remember, calling on the Name of God represents His attributes – so it's perfectly all right to reference His attributes in connection with Who He is. I think of these as "divine nicknames," subheadings that also connect us to the essence of God's purpose. Whenever we are in a relationship with someone, we know who they are and we associate who they are and our regards and interaction with them by their name, their nickname, or even by description. Most of us have immediate responses when we hear a name, whether that response is positive or negative. The same is true no matter how we call upon God, and how we live to honor our relationship with Him.

All effective prayer begins by praising God for all He is and in all His power and praising God in His Name through the Name of Jesus Christ. This is the most effective way we can praise God for all He is.

Our God, we thank You
  and praise Your wonderful Name. (1 Chronicles 29:13)

To praise the Name of God means:

- We praise all God has ever done
- We praise all God ever will do
- We praise all God is now doing, even if we don't know what that may be
- We praise His supremacy and His grandeur
- We reaffirm our need for Him

Praising God is the cornerstone to prayer, because through it, we identify Him in glory and ourselves in humility. Praising God's Name can be done through song, through reading Scriptures praising His Name, or even just speaking words of praise to God for all He has done.

PRAY FOR KINGDOM MATTERS

When was the last time you prayed for missionaries? For spiritual leaders, beyond your own? For people to come into the Kingdom, and for the proper foundations to be present to turn converts into disciples? Have you ever prayed, not just for people to come into the Kingdom, but for workers to do the work of the Kingdom? Is Kingdom financing a part of your regular prayers? Do you remember to pray for matters affecting the Kingdom of God?

Admittedly, many of us don't. We're often overly caught up in problems we face or needs we have. Because we don't often take the proper time for prayer, we rush through it, focusing on what's most immediate and important to us. This is common, but a mistake. If we rush through prayer, we don't consider the communication and relationship aspects of it. When it comes to prayer for Kingdom matters, this is where prayer just doesn't connect us to God. It also connects us to other believers.

When I am contacted by other ministries via social media, one of my biggest complaints is that their only interests are for me to either pray for them and their needs or to do something for them. Very seldom does someone come to me and ask if I, or my ministry, have any requests or needs. This tells me two things. The first is that whoever is contacting me is very concerned with themselves. The second is that their scope is so limited, they are not really Kingdom minded (no matter how many times they might use the word "Kingdom" in a sentence). If we can't consider others and we certainly don't think about remembering others in prayer, then we need to do better when it comes to honoring and walking in the work of the Kingdom. Praying for Kingdom matters is a great place to start.

In Kingdom matters, we are not worried about our laundry list of issues, personal needs, and feelings. We are concerned about, first, and before all things, the Kingdom of God to which we are a part. After all, it is this Kingdom that changes our worldly perspective, bringing it into eternity. Everything we see right now and continue to experience will change and transform with time. Temporal things come and go, pass and continue. It's essential we keep sight of where we are and what we are appointed to do, and we also remember the bigger picture of our purpose and calling in this life. In praying for the Kingdom, we are establishing ourselves as a part of something greater, this Kingdom of God that expanses heaven and earth.

But first, be concerned about His Kingdom and what has His approval. Then all these things will be provided for you. (Matthew 6:33)

When praying for matters, Kingdom issues must come first. The advance of God's Kingdom is our priority. If we seek God's Kingdom first, we can trust that God will take care of all our needs in Christ Jesus and we can go on as faithful stewards with the Gospel, living our lives every day according to Kingdom principles. We should pray for the Kingdom before ourselves, because the Kingdom is our first concern. In praying for the Kingdom, we pray for:

- God's Kingdom spread out over the earth
- The advance, structure, and implementation of God's Kingdom
- Missionaries and missions
- The purpose of God's Kingdom
- The leadership of God's Kingdom
- The integrity of those who are sent into the harvest
- Disciples of all age groups, nations, and positions on their spiritual walk
- Wisdom, insight, and knowledge for those who claim to be of Christ

- Those who are preparing to take new steps into Kingdom advancement and leadership
- Provision for all who are part of God's Kingdom
- Known needs of others in the Kingdom
- Unspoken needs of others in the Kingdom

PRAY FOR NECESSITIES

I meet many people who desire for me to join or agree in prayer with them for things that are above and beyond the call of necessities. As an example, perhaps the most common request I receive is for someone to find a wife or husband. Secondly, someone wants their spouse or family members to line up the way they desire. Beyond this, we find requests for "bigger" things: a bigger or better house or car, a boat, moving to a more expensive neighborhood, or "increase" in some area of their lives.

It's important to state that none of these things are necessities. They are things we want, oftentimes desires of our flesh rather than the Spirit. The fact that I receive these requests proves two things. The first is that we are very in touch with our wants. The second is that we aren't very connected to our needs. There's a definite blur between these two lines, as it becomes a matter of what one thinks God should (or is obligated) to do for them.

I don't think there's anything wrong with wanting to move up in life. God, however, asks that we are more in touch with need than want, especially when it comes to prayer. As we sit and stew in the things we want, there is someone in the world who doesn't have enough to eat, clean water, shoes to wear, or school to attend. No, we can't fix poverty by ourselves, but we can start by developing a prayer life that focuses on needs rather than wants, opening the door for a greater sense of spiritual gratitude.

As I am working on the revision of this text, much of the western world faces financial shortage. Decades of looking to the government for our needs rather than God has led to idolatry, and we are left with sky-high prices and wages that don't meet our needs. Rather than seeking God for more, we should look to God for practical life matters, making our priority need rather than want.

In focusing first on need and then want, it creates a different outlook on life. Knowledge of need keeps us from greed and from excessive want. It provides us with the grace to make ourselves aware of the need for moderation when applicable. God shows us how to make what we have enough and blesses us abundantly as we grow to recognize His presence in our lives through divine provision.

This issue of need vs. want in prayer raises an important question: what do we really need in our life? Jesus gives us an example of need in Matthew 6: We need daily bread, or physical nourishment. This could be classified as a statement to cover all our regular needs for survival. We need food, shelter, water, clothing and shoes. We need to have basic needs met, so that we may continue in our callings and make them fruitful. We need companionship, fellowship, and community, we need emotional health and mental stability, and we need love, particularly the love of God that transforms us. Beyond that, all things unnecessary for living become wants.

It's not wrong to have wants or to pray that God gives us certain things, whether it's showing us His favor or that He blesses us in some specific way in our lives. It's certainly not wrong, at all. It is certainly wrong to want so much that we lose sight of need when so many of this world live in a perpetual state of unmet needs.

Everyone in the world is concerned about these things, but your Father knows you need them. (Luke 12:30)

In prayer, we cast our needs upon God, knowing that He shall meet all our needs according to His riches and glory in Christ Jesus. Everyone in the world has concerns about needs and having their needs met, but only those who truly rely on God and His faithfulness to meet our needs has the assurance that those things shall be met. We might not understand how He does everything or by what means He does it, but we are always able to trust that He will. Giving our necessities to God gives us the freedom to focus even more on His work in this world and His plan for our lives. It's as simple as that: we can trust Him and move forward with our assignment, whatever that might be.

PRAY FOR FORGIVENESS

We will discuss forgiveness a little more in-depth later in this book. We will speak on it a little bit here because it is an integral part of prayer. Forgiveness is one of those topics we can't hear enough about. Unfortunately, we don't hear about it often. Sure, we like to talk about forgiveness in terms of our salvation and of being forgiven from all our sins. We don't like to hear that we will sin again and will have to ask for forgiveness, or that others will offend or sin against us and we will have to forgive them, as well. Forgiveness is not a one-time event; it is a lifelong work, a graceful manifestation that will arise multiple times throughout your life. We will continually require forgiveness, both to receive and give, and as a result, it is a primary element of prayer.

Forgiveness is a fundamental aspect of our faith. Without forgiveness, we have nothing and are nothing, and we live without any semblance of hope. Because we are forgiven, we are able to walk in that forgiveness and offer forgiveness for the offenses of others. We also can walk through life free, thanks to it: free from the shame and guilt of what we have done in the past, free from the hurts that come our way, free from the intimidation or opinions others that harm us as people, and a general loosing to follow the work of God rather than being bound to what we see right now and what we experience in the future.

As we go through life, forgiveness will be something we will continually require, both from others and for others, not to mention the forgiveness we need from God. Forgiveness is a primary element of prayer as it is the very foundation of our faith. We can forgive, because we know we are forgiven by God through Christ. Why not make forgiveness a daily practice? Every day, ask God to forgive you for what you have done wrong, and ask God to forgive others for their wrongdoings toward you.

Be kind to each other, sympathetic, forgiving each other as God has forgiven you through Christ. (Ephesians 4:32)

Forgiveness is always relevant; always important; always in style; and always for prayer. The more in touch we are to pray for forgiveness, the more in touch we are with the heart of God, and the relevance of being forgiven, rather than it being a mere musing that we like to talk about on holidays and salvation anniversaries. Praying for forgiveness makes it an applicable, everyday part of one's faith walk and spiritual experience.

PRAY TO RESIST TEMPTATIONS

We already tapped on the issue of temptation when we spoke about finances earlier in this book. Financial temptations aren't the only ones we need to be aware of, however. I have often said that life is tempting, and one of the major keys to success in life (no matter what one may believe) is learning to live with temptation. We can try to avoid temptations, we can try to circumvent them, we can try to pretend they don't exist, but the best way to handle temptation is to acknowledge it exists and live with the fact that some things are tempting to us. With God's help, we can resist temptation, and gain that much more victory over whatever tries to come against us.

Let's define temptation as personal challenges that arise to try and sway us in a certain direction. We usually understand temptation to mean that something might pull us away from our faith, but we can be tempted to handle or to deal with anything. Temptation represents places of weakness in our lives, issues we have that have either left a metaphorical open door for something else to come in or they are things that call to us in a way that cause us harm or are simply bad for us. There are many reasons why temptation may arise in one's life; it is not a simple matter of saying people do things to merit temptation or that they bring it upon themselves. If you are alive, if you are breathing, there are things that you will be tempted to do at some point in time. They might be different than someone else's temptations, but they will be there, nonetheless, as everyone's got something.

Through many years of ministry, I have come to caution people against outright saying there are things they will "never" do, because those are often the things that come tempting us, knocking down our door in difficult times. I don't have a deep, spiritual explanation for why these become the very things that tempt us, beyond the fact that if we've decided something will never be an issue for us, we aren't watching for the signs that something may become an issue for us. If we aren't prepared, that means when the temptation rises, we won't be ready to resist it.

Too many come into the Christian life thinking their faith will ensure they are never tempted again. Just because we are Christian does not mean every temptation of life magically goes away, so we can be more comfortable. Second to wants, I believe the most commonly prayed prayers are not for endurance and strength against temptation, but to be removed from temptation's difficulties and challenges. Many prayers people pray go something like the following: "Lord, please make so-and-so do what I want" or "God, do what I want!" Prayer is not like that at all! We don't pray so God can fix everyone else or make our circumstances easy. It's fine to pray for others or to ask God to intervene in someone's life, but it isn't right for us to be demanding in prayer that God conform to our will so we can be comfortable.

Temptation rises when things don't go our way: people don't do what we want, we aren't happy in our lives, we don't connect with others like we'd hoped we would; we don't make decisions about relationships that will enhance our blessing; and life becomes stressful, miserable, or challenging. A basic reality of life is that things will not always go our way, nor will we always like life's outcomes. People and circumstances will both prove trying, tempting, and difficult. We will find ourselves faced with choices and opportunities to engage in various temptations and to avoid doing what we know is right to change a situation for the better. What should we do? Pray, even before temptation comes upon us!

My brothers and sisters, be very happy when you are tested in different ways. You know that such testing of your faith produces endurance. (James 1:2-3)

As people, we should pray for grace to go through what we need to go through and make necessary changes when issues arise. Things will come up as we go through this life, and we shouldn't be caught off guard because we've been praying for the wrong things or limiting our prayers to material wants. Temptations are time to grow in grace. Whether we resist temptation or have to find our way back to God's grace after the fact, we are able to see the work of God in our lives and will come out a little bit stronger for the next time. We grow when we see God work for us in our temptations and we gain a great victory when we use prayer as a weapon when it comes to handling temptation.

PRAY FOR ALL THAT BELONGS TO GOD

We know the Kingdom, the power, and the glory belong to God from reading the Scriptures. Do we remember to pray for all that belongs to God, and that we can reflect all that belongs to God? What is this, you ask? It's everything, because everything, in the end, belongs to God!

Nor will people say, Look! Here [it is]! or, See, [it is] there! For behold, the kingdom of God is within you [in your hearts] and among you [surrounding you]. (Luke 17:21, AMPC)

We, right here, right now, are a part of all that belongs to God! We have two ways of looking at our lives: we can either see us as infinitesimally small and irrelevant, or we can see ourselves as a part of something much bigger and much greater than we are. We aren't by ourselves, even though it might feel that way some of the time. We are a part of this big, great plan. We have the opportunity to live our part of God's plan to the fullest. How do we discern this plan? Through prayer!

Everything about our lives should echo the Kingdom of God, the promise of eternity living within us. What we do and what we pray, therefore, should reflect this important, living promise. In praying for all that belongs to God, we pray for ourselves:

- To receive the strength to live for the Kingdom every day, and in every way
- To be better positioned to walk in, represent, and receive whatever God has for us
- To accept His will and live out that will in our lives
- To know God better, seeing Him revealed to us in a deeper way
- To be properly equipped to do Kingdom work

We also pray for:

- Wisdom for world leaders
- Citizens of this world
- The evangelism of all nations
- Peace and justice
- Equity among citizens
- Fair distribution and responsible use of natural resources
- Answers to the world's social issues
- Any other matter that is pressing as is found under heaven

 As representatives who belong to God, let's pray with fervency to walk through each day, bringing glory to the power and grace of His Kingdom. Such intent in prayers also reminds us to pray for all those who live and work in God's Kingdom and to support our brothers and sisters in Christ through edification.

ADJUSTING OUR CONCEPT OF ANSWERED PRAYER

Whenever you start talking about prayer, issues arise within hearts and minds. One of the most common issues is that of unanswered prayer, or what we perceive to be unanswered prayer. Feeling as if we have something that has been unfavorably answered by God – or not answered at all – through prayer can be a very difficult thing to experience. It can cause us to think God does not care about us or is not responsive to our needs. We might have trouble trying to figure out what to do or how to handle any given situation, and the waiting may arise various feelings of confusion, anger, frustration, and even abandoned faith.

How we approach unanswered prayer relates to our level of spiritual maturity. In this same vain, we can't mature spiritually in any issue if we are not properly taught. Unanswered prayer is often untouched because people don't know how to teach on it. Leaders also wrestle with questions of unanswered prayer. If they are wrestling with it themselves, they might not feel qualified to examine it from the pulpit. If we've grown up with enough faith education to know about prayer but not to know about the mechanics and underlying nature of prayer itself, we are going to find ourselves confounded and confused much of the time.

In talking about unanswered prayers, there are two main memories I have that come to mind. One was when my mom was in contact with someone she hadn't spoken to in many, many years who seemed to be plagued with many, many problems. Whatever those problems were is unknown, because she would raise the issue of them, but she refused to elaborate. She was very quick to make it clear, however, that part of her issues with faith and with God were the facts that so many of her prayers had gone unanswered. Whenever that issue was addressed, and my mom would try to talk about her issues with her faith, she would quickly shut down.

On another occasion, I met a woman seeking healing at a conference I attended. I was not the main speaker, but someone asked me to assist after the service was over with prayer for this woman's healing. It was obvious the woman was quite resistant to receive what was said to her, and we came to discover she was not a Christian and was antithetical to faith in many ways. One of her arguments was that prayer was meaningless, because whatever was going to happen was going to happen, and that prayer couldn't change anything.

What I would say to both women is the same, even though their circumstances are a bit different. It's true that we might pray and the situation we are in may not change at all. Things may stay exactly the same. But the purposes of prayer are relationship and communication, not getting what we want all the time. Prayer is supposed to help us grow and transform and gain greater insight into God and our walk with Him. While prayer might not change the immediacy of our situations all the time (although it can), it can change us. Through prayer, we can communicate with God and find a way to better handle what we are going through, or see it from a different perspective, or maybe even see ourselves in it differently. Prayers open the door for us to see a way through, get through what we must go through, or see things from another angle. Prayer might not change our situations, but it always, without a doubt, has the ability to change us.

Jesus used this illustration with his disciples to show them that they need to pray all the time and never give up. He said, "In a city there was a judge who didn't fear God or respect people. In that city there was also a widow who kept coming to him and saying, 'Give me justice.'

"For a while the judge refused to do anything. But then he thought, 'This widow really annoys me. Although I don't fear God or respect people, I'll have to give her justice. Otherwise, she'll keep coming to me until she wears me out.'"

The Lord added, "Pay attention to what the dishonest judge thought. Won't God give His chosen people justice when they cry out to Him for help day and night? Is He slow to help them? I can guarantee that He will give them justice quickly. But when the Son of Man comes, will He find faith on earth?" (Luke 18:1-8)

There is no doubt and no question that unanswered prayer might be hard to handle. Sometimes unanswered prayer isn't so much unanswered as it's not the answer that we want. There can be many reasons for this. We aren't seeing things from God's perspective and with His insight, and prayer can serve a powerful way to gain knowledge of our Creator and the way He sees and embraces our situations. Maybe what we seek just isn't right for us, or what we need right now, or maybe the timing is just not right. It's possible that God has something else for us, all together. Maybe through our trial, He is trying to get our attention. Maybe what we request is simply not of God. Maybe we are harboring unforgiveness or bitterness, and our request reflects this in what we request or our motive. Maybe things are the way they are, just because that's how it is right now. We don't know and will never find out if we are unwilling to pray our way through, seeking His face and His knowledge as we navigate through an unfamiliar – and uncomfortable – situation.

TYPES OF PRAYER

If you look up "types of prayer" online, you will find blogs, writings, sites, podcasts, and postings about prayer, telling you long lists of prayer and embellishing on types of prayer. Anyone can try and expound upon different prayers as are seen in the Scriptures and give them new headings, but there are only a few different forms of prayer, which we will look at here, to help you pray more effectively and come into a place of the will of God for you, in your life.

- **Praise:** Prayer offering that focuses exclusively on God. It exists to honor Him and laud the fullness of what He has done (Psalm 95:1-6).

- **Worship:** Prayer offering that focuses exclusively on God. It exists to honor Him and thank Him for Who He Is. Beyond these points, it exists to honor and dwell in His presence (Luke 11:2-4).

- **Prayer of faith:** Prayer communicated to God in and through faith, with full assurance that God shall do exactly what one has believed – and prayed to receive. Such prayer communicates belief in God's ability. By praying a prayer of faith, one ideally comes into a better understanding of the will of God (James 5:15).

- **Prayer of consecration:** Prayer that establishes an agreement with the will of God, submitting oneself to God's will, even when it is hard or difficult (Matthew 26:39).

- **Group prayer:** Also called public or corporate prayer, when a group comes together for prayer to touch and agree on behalf of all needs present, and to do the work of God (Acts 1:14, Acts 2:42).

- **Private prayer:** Prayer between an individual in God, prayed without the assistance of anyone else (Matthew 6:5-6).

- **Prayer of thanksgiving:** Prayer that thanks God for all that He is and all that He has done (Philippians 4:6).

- **Supplications:** Prayer made in humility and honesty, making a petition before God (1 Timothy 2:1).

- **Intercessory prayer:** Prayer on behalf of others, imploring on behalf of heaven and earth. More than just praying a list of prayers, intercessors literally wrangle, to stand in the gap for the needs that exist, both on earth and in heaven (1 Timothy 2:1).

<u>PRAYING THE SCRIPTURES</u>

Many ask if, considering the will of God for our lives, it is all right to pray the traditional prayers we always have, such as the literal words of the Our Father prayer. There is nothing wrong with praying any of the literal words found in Scripture. In fact, speaking the Scriptures is a powerful form of prayer that recalls how God has helped others in the past, and how He can come through for us, even now. Below are a few Scriptural prayers (found in the Psalms) that are powerful for your prayer. As you develop a greater heart for the Scriptures, I am sure you will find others that speak to you in times of prayer.

I will thank the Lord at all times.
  My mouth will always praise Him.
My soul will boast about the Lord.
  Those who are oppressed will hear it and rejoice.
Praise the Lord's greatness with me.
Let us highly honor His Name together.
I went to the Lord for help.
  He answered me and rescued me from all my fears.
All who look to Him will be radiant.
  Their faces will never be covered with shame.
Here is a poor man who called out.
  The Lord heard him and saved him from all his troubles.
The Messenger of the Lord camps around those who fear Him,
  and he rescues them.
Taste and see that the Lord is good.
  Blessed is the person who takes refuge in Him.
Fear the Lord, you holy people who belong to Him.
  Those who fear Him are never in need. (Psalm 34:1-9)

Have pity on me, O God, in keeping with Your mercy.
  In keeping with Your unlimited compassion, wipe out my rebellious acts.
Wash me thoroughly from my guilt,
  and cleanse me from my sin.
    I admit that I am rebellious.
    My sin is always in front of me.
I have sinned against You, especially You.
I have done what You consider evil.
  So You hand down justice when You speak,
  and You are blameless when You judge.

Indeed, I was born guilty.
  I was a sinner when my mother conceived me.
Yet, You desire truth and sincerity.
  Deep down inside me You teach me wisdom.
Purify me from sin with hyssop, and I will be clean.
Wash me, and I will be whiter than snow.
  Let me hear sounds of joy and gladness.
  Let the bones that You have broken dance.
Hide Your face from my sins,
  and wipe out all that I have done wrong.

Create a clean heart in me, O God,
  and renew a faithful spirit within me.
Do not force me away from Your presence,
  and do not take Your Holy Spirit from me.
Restore the joy of Your salvation to me,
  and provide me with a spirit of willing obedience.

Then I will teach Your ways to those who are rebellious,
  and sinners will return to You.
Rescue me from the guilt of murder,
  O God, my savior.
Let my tongue sing joyfully about Your righteousness!
O Lord, open my lips,
  and my mouth will tell about Your praise.
You are not happy with any sacrifice.
  Otherwise, I would offer one to You.
You are not pleased with burnt offerings.
  The sacrifice pleasing to God is a broken spirit.
  O God, You do not despise a broken and sorrowful heart.
Favor Zion with Your goodness.
Rebuild the walls of Jerusalem.
  Then You will be pleased with sacrifices offered in the right spirit—
    with burnt offerings and whole burnt offerings.
      Young bulls will be offered on Your altar. (Psalm 51:1-19)

Whoever lives under the shelter of the Most High
  will remain in the shadow of the Almighty.
I will say to the Lord,
  "You are my refuge and my fortress, my God in Whom I trust."

He is the One Who will rescue you from hunters' traps
and from deadly plagues.
He will cover you with his feathers,
and under His wings you will find refuge.
His truth is your shield and armor.

You do not need to fear
terrors of the night,
arrows that fly during the day,
plagues that roam the dark,
epidemics that strike at noon.
They will not come near you,
even though a thousand may fall dead beside you
or ten thousand at your right side.

You only have to look with your eyes
to see the punishment of wicked people.

You, O Lord, are my refuge!
You have made the Most High your home.
No harm will come to you.
No sickness will come near your house.
He will put His angels in charge of you
to protect you in all your ways.
They will carry you in their hands
so that you never hit your foot against a rock.
You will step on lions and cobras.
You will trample young lions and snakes.

Because you love Me, I will rescue you.
I will protect you because you know My Name.
When you call to Me, I will answer you.
I will be with you when you are in trouble.
I will save you and honor you.
I will satisfy you with a long life.
I will show you how I will save you. (Psalm 91:1-16)

Give thanks to the Lord because He is good,
because His mercy endures forever.
Israel should say,
"His mercy endures forever."

The descendants of Aaron should say,
"His mercy endures forever."
Those who fear the Lord should say,
"His mercy endures forever."

During times of trouble I called on the Lord.
The Lord answered me and set me free from all of them.
The Lord is on my side.
I am not afraid.
What can mortals do to me?
The Lord is on my side as my helper.
I will see the defeat of those who hate me.
It is better to depend on the Lord
than to trust mortals.
It is better to depend on the Lord
than to trust influential people.

All the nations surrounded me,
but armed with the Name of the Lord, I defeated them.
They surrounded me. Yes, they surrounded me,
but armed with the Name of the Lord, I defeated them.
They swarmed around me like bees,
but they were extinguished like burning thornbushes.
So armed with the Name of the Lord, I defeated them.
They pushed hard to make me fall,
but the Lord helped me.
The Lord is my strength and my song.
He is my Savior.

The sound of joyful singing and victory is heard
in the tents of righteous people.
The right hand of the Lord displays strength.
The right hand of the Lord is held high.
The right hand of the Lord displays strength.
I will not die,
but I will live and tell what the Lord has done.
The Lord disciplined me severely,
but He did not allow me to be killed.

Open the gates of righteousness for me.
I will go through them and give thanks to the Lord.

This is the gate of the Lord
through which righteous people will enter.

I give thanks to You,
because You have answered me.
You are my Savior.
The stone that the builders rejected
has become the cornerstone.
The Lord is responsible for this,
and it is amazing for us to see.
This is the day the Lord has made.
Let's rejoice and be glad today!
We beg you, O Lord, save us!
We beg you, O Lord, give us success!
Blessed is the One Who comes in the Name of the Lord.
We bless You from the Lord's house.
The Lord is God, and He has given us light.
March in a festival procession
with branches to the horns of the altar.
You are my God, and I give thanks to You.
My God, I honor You highly.

Give thanks to the Lord because He is good,
because His mercy endures forever. (Psalm 118:1-29)

"From the time I was young, people have attacked me ..."
(Israel should repeat this.)
"From the time I was young, people have attacked me,
but they have never overpowered me.
They have plowed my back like farmers plow fields.
They made long slashes like furrows."
The Lord is righteous.
He has cut me loose
from the ropes that wicked people tied around me.
Put to shame all those who hate Zion.
Force them to retreat.
Make them be like grass on a roof,
like grass that dries up before it produces a stalk.
It will never fill the barns of those who harvest
or the arms of those who gather bundles.
Those who pass by will never say to them,

"May you be blessed by the Lord"
   or "We bless you in the name of the Lord." (Psalm 129:1-8)

See how good and pleasant it is
   when brothers and sisters live together in harmony!
   It is like fine, scented oil on the head,
   running down the beard—down Aaron's beard—
   running over the collar of his robes.
   It is like dew on Mount Hermon,
   dew which comes down on Zion's mountains.
That is where the Lord promised
   the blessing of eternal life. (Psalm 133:1-3)

Praise the Lord, all you servants of the Lord,
   all who stand in the house of the Lord night after night.
Lift your hands toward the holy place, and praise the Lord.
May the Lord, the maker of heaven and earth, bless you from Zion. (Psalm 134:1-3)

I will give thanks to You with all my heart.
   I will make music to praise You in front of the false gods.
I will bow toward Your holy temple.
I will give thanks to Your Name because of Your mercy and truth.
You have made Your Name and Your promise greater than everything.

When I called, You answered me.
   You made me bold by strengthening my soul.
All the kings of the earth will give thanks to You, O Lord,
   because they have heard the promises You spoke.
   They will sing this about the ways of the Lord:
   "The Lord's honor is great!"
Even though the Lord is high above, He sees humble people close up,
   and He recognizes arrogant people from a distance.

Even though I walk into the middle of trouble,
   You guard my life against the anger of my enemies.
   You stretch out your hand,
   and Your right hand saves me.
The Lord will do everything for me.
   O Lord, your mercy endures forever.
   Do not let go of what your hands have made. (Psalm 138:1-8)

Loudly, I cry to the Lord.
  Loudly, I plead with the Lord for mercy.
I pour out my complaints in his presence
  and tell Him my troubles.
When I begin to lose hope,
  You already know what I am experiencing.

My enemies have hidden a trap for me on the path where I walk.
  Look to my right and see that no one notices me.
  Escape is impossible for me.
  No one cares about me.

I call out to You, O Lord.
  I say, "You are my refuge,
  my own inheritance in this world of the living."
  Pay attention to my cry for help
  because I am very weak.
Rescue me from those who pursue me
  because they are too strong for me.
Release my soul from prison
  so that I may give thanks to Your Name.
Righteous people will surround me
  because You are good to me. (Psalm 142:1-7)

O Lord, listen to my prayer.
  Open Your ears to hear my urgent requests.
  Answer me because You are faithful and righteous.
Do not take me to court for judgment,
  because there is no one alive
  who is righteous in Your presence.

The enemy has pursued me.
  He has ground my life into the dirt.
  He has made me live in dark places
  like those who have died long ago.
That is why I begin to lose hope
  and my heart is in a state of shock.

I remember the days long ago.
  I reflect on all that You have done.
  I carefully consider what Your hands have made.

I stretch out my hands to You in prayer.
　Like parched land, my soul thirsts for You. Selah

Answer me quickly, O Lord.
　My spirit is worn out.
　Do not hide Your face from me,
　　or I will be like those who go into the pit.
　Let me hear about Your mercy in the morning,
　　because I trust You.
Let me know the way that I should go,
because I long for You.
Rescue me from my enemies, O Lord.
　I come to You for protection.

Teach me to do Your will, because You are my God.
　May Your good Spirit lead me on level ground.
O Lord, keep me alive for the sake of Your Name.
　Because You are righteous, lead me out of trouble.
In keeping with your mercy, wipe out my enemies
　and destroy all who torment me,
　　because I am Your servant. (Psalm 143:1-12)

Hallelujah!

Praise the Lord from the heavens.
Praise Him in the heights above.
Praise Him, all His angels.
Praise Him, His entire heavenly army.
Praise Him, sun and moon.
Praise Him, all shining stars.
Praise him, you highest heaven
　and the water above the sky.
Let them praise the Name of the Lord
　because they were created by His command.
He set them in their places forever and ever.
He made it a law that no one can break.

Praise the Lord from the earth.
Praise Him, large sea creatures and all the ocean depths,
　lightning and hail,
　snow and fog,

strong winds that obey His commands,
mountains and all hills,
fruit trees and all cedar trees,
wild animals and all domestic animals,
crawling animals and birds,
kings of the earth and all its people,
officials and all judges on the earth,
young men and women,
old and young together.
Let them praise the Name of the Lord
because His Name is high above all others.
His glory is above heaven and earth.
He has given His people a strong leader,
someone praiseworthy for His faithful ones,
for the people of Israel, the people who are close to Him.

Hallelujah! (Psalm 148:1-14)

<u>Hearing from God</u>

Unlike some of my counterparts, I firmly believe God speaks to us today. If we are in a relationship with someone, it is only natural they communicate with us through speech. If we talk to God, God will talk to us. Speech isn't the only way we communicate, however. We also communicate through body language, gestures, signs, messages, and many other methods that are what we might classify as non-verbal. This means that in our relationship with God, we aren't going to expect to only hear from God verbally all the time. There are many ways we might hear from God and experience His presence in our lives, just as is the case when we are in a relationship with others, as well.

Whenever we read the Bible and it talks about someone "hearing from God" or "the Lord came to" so-and-so, what do you think happened? Do you have images in your head of God sitting down with someone over a cup of tea and revealing His will to them? Is it more of a getting hit with a lightning bolt kind of deal, or maybe God whispering in someone's ear? Odds are good (in fact I'd say with all certainty) that this is not, in any way, how God ever spoke to anyone. There are a few ways God has spoken that we can identify, and we can trust that God still speaks by those means, even now.

- **Audibly:** This indicates someone hears God's voice, in a literal sense. How this happens or by what means, it's difficult to describe, but those who have had this experience can vouch when they hear an audible voice (usually a quiet voice) within a situation (Acts 9:4-5).

- **Angelic encounters:** Angels have appeared throughout history as God's messengers, beings who come from heaven to send us word down here on earth. While our angelic encounters might not always be as cut and dry or as dramatic as some we see in Scripture, there are angels among us and around us, with a message from heaven (Luke 1:26-28, Hebrews 13:2).

- **Nature:** God speaks to us through not just the beauty of creation, but also when things go naturally awry or are out of order. When something out of the ordinary happened in the ancient world (such as famine or drought), the first thing the people did was call for a sacred assembly and spiritual fast. This was so they could discern God's voice in the situation (Psalm 19:1-2, Romans 1:20).

- **The inner voice (sometimes called witness) of the Holy Spirit:** Some refer to this as an instinct, a knowing, or a spiritual conviction, it is an instance where God gives guidance within an individual's soul via the Holy Spirit. It is used to provide direct guidance (1 Kings 19:12, John 14:26, Acts 11:12, 1 Corinthians 3:16).

- **Dreams, signs, and visions:** Sometimes when God speaks to us, He may speak through a dream, a sign, or a vision, all of which communicate a supernatural message. It might not always be clear what it means as there might be symbols involved in its transmission, but dreams, signs, and visions are a powerful – and common way – God communicates with His people (Matthew 1:20-21, Acts 2:17-20, Acts 10:9-18).

- **Prophecy:** Prophecy is not just a ministry office, but also a spiritual gift that stands when an individual speaks the thoughts and words of God (1 Corinthians 12:10).

- **Word of wisdom/word of knowledge:** Both a word of wisdom and a word of knowledge are examples of spiritual gifts that provide us a word in due season from God through another person. A word of wisdom reflects advice, caution or insight, while a word of knowledge provides divine information into or about a situation (1 Corinthians 12:8, Hebrews 6:13-20).

- **Wise counsel:** It's amazing how God can provide a word in due season through the counsel of those who hear from God and are able to offer wisdom in any given situation (Proverbs 12:15).

- **Difficulties:** We don't enjoy difficulties by any stretch of the imagination, but difficulties are a way that God speaks to us (Psalm 119:67-68).

- **Whoever God so desires to speak through:** God can speak through whomever He so desires, whenever He so desires (Job 33:14).

- **Scripture:** If we believe in the inspiration of the Scriptures, that means we believe they contain God-breathed words that can fill us with things God wants us to hear, know, and provide us with guidance and comfort (Psalm 119:11, 2 Timothy 3:16).

If we want to hear from God, we need to take the mystery out of the process and start looking over the list above to discern the ways God is speaking to us and what He is saying in our lives. We must make the commitment to stop ignoring the inward witnesses, the voice, the signs, and the sound of God's presence in our lives and start embracing it in a way that directs us to the place where we need to be. Developing our relationship with God and getting it to a solid place requires us to listen at least as much, if not more, than we speak, to watch and observe as much as we act, and to abide in patience, especially when we are uncertain about the answers. God always provides us an answer, and He always speaks, but we must be willing to pay attention and accept the answers we receive as we trust God's eternal foresight.

Just as communication with other people can prove to build us up, so too does prayer edify our relationship with God. Prayer is not a chore we engage in so we will keep a distant deity happy. It is something we do because we love God and desire to know Him better and deeper in our lives. Through prayer, we speak, and we listen, we observe, and we give, we purpose our hearts for what is coming, and we learn and fellowship from God Himself. Our prayer life is a relationship exercise, meant to be a refresher and edifier of everything good, noble, and spiritual. Through prayer, we tie our physical lives and realities to our spiritual lives and realities. The spiritual realm isn't beyond our reach; it is as near and as close to us as our next prayer. God isn't quite as distant as many proclaim Him to be, and what a gift prayer is to us that we can communicate and talk to God at any time: in good seasons and in bad, in times of plenty and lean times, and in praise and cries for help. No matter what we are doing or where we are, we can always communicate with God via the means of prayer.

Never stop praying. (1 Thessalonians 5:17)

The command to pray without ceasing might sound intimidating, but the very essence of it is the answer to the way that prayer transforms our very relationship and identity with God. In everything we do, we are communicating with God through prayer, praise, obedience, and action. Our very lives reflect the way in which we are connected to God, and He is at the center of our lives. The sooner we realize this, the sooner we will embrace the ideal that being a part of the Kingdom and being in Christ means being in prayer with God, earnestly, and without ceasing.

The prayer of Jabez was all the rage a few years back because an author wrote a devotional series of books based on this short, few-line prayer located in what many would consider an obscure section of the Scriptures (it's found in the middle of a long genealogical passage of 1 Chronicles). It took off as a wildfire trend because everyone liked noting that Jabez's prayer was answered by God. We loved the idea that some obscure guy said a few short lines and got exactly what he wanted, and that we can do the same if we tap into his unique formula. The problem is, there wasn't a formula; Jabez was praying from his heart.

Jabez was more honorable than his brothers. His mother had named him Jabez [Painful], because she said that his birth was painful. Jabez prayed to the God of Israel, "Please bless me and give me more territory. May Your power be with me and free me from evil so that I will not be in pain." God gave him what he prayed for. (1 Chronicles 4:9-10)

Jabez's prayer gives us insight into a heart that God uses through prayer. Jabez was so named because his birth was painful. What an awful stigma that must have been to walk around with throughout his life. Imagine having to have a name that is a constant reminder of something about yourself that you really couldn't control, but inflicted discomfort on someone else. (Keep that in mind next time you complain about your given name!) This didn't identify Jabez, however, in a negative way. He didn't walk around his entire life feeling sorry for himself or feeling guilty. In fact, the Scriptures reveal to us that Jabez was more honorable than his brothers, despite the identity he had. He made the point to be an honorable man, to do right before God and others, and maintained that as a center point in his life.

Jabez's prayer was answered by God because Jabez was in the center of God's will for his life. He knew who he was, and he knew what he needed to maintain the balance of an evil-free and pain-free life. In his prayer, Jabez wasn't selfish. He was placing himself in God's hands, as pain was associated with wrongdoing or evil and an increase in territory would create more opportunities to do right. He wanted his life to operate by God's hand and God's will, and He knew the only way was to allow God to move in his life, give him more of a scope, move him by His power, and keep him from evil, all the days of his life.

There are so many examples of prayer in the Scriptures, but Jabez is special because he shows us the way to effective prayer. We need to pray with the heart of Jabez. In prayer, it becomes less about us and more about uniting ourselves with God's will. As we communicate with God, He shows us more of Himself, and we, in turn, respond to that with open arms as we transform ourselves. Never underestimate the power of prayer. It might not always get you what you think you want, but it will land you in the place you need: right in the heart of God.

(5)
HE MUST INCREASE, BUT I MUST DECREASE

The fear of the Lord is discipline leading to wisdom,
and humility comes before honor.
(Proverbs 15:33)

God increasing within us and our decreasing flesh aren't central aspects of the Gospel message that we like to hear. John 3:30 is a verse that we probably drift past, not considering what it says or what it means in our lives. It's just seen as another verse that proves Who Jesus was, right? We don't give much thought to what it means for us, in the here and now, and that there is a powerful spiritual principle present in the words of John the Baptist in that verse.

Many of us like the idea of being successful, but we haven't quite come to a place where we understand what "success" is. Historically speaking, people had a far different understanding of what it meant to be successful than we do now. If they raised their families to adulthood and were able to maintain their households, people considered themselves relatively successful. Now we think success is based on our income, our jobs, our social status, how famous we are, and how in tune everyone around us is with where we are and what we want to do.

Doing God's work means we are humble enough to let God into our lives, let God work, and let God become a part of our lives. The goal is to display His nature more, and our fleshly behavior less. This can sound a lot easier – and a lot more fun – than it really is. When we are first believers, everything (and I do mean everything) seems new and different, and it is all about God. We don't want it to be about us, because that might somehow dampen our witness and change our level of interest. As we discussed earlier, however, this thrill wanes. It will probably return when breakthroughs are reached or changes are made for periods of time, but the maintenance of life often gets in the way of our focus on the things of God. This is where humility and success often intersect, and unfortunately, it's not always pretty when they meet. Our demands for success often squash our desires for humility. In the process of drive and desire, we often lose our true focus for the Kingdom and all that comes with it.

However, we don't want to admit this. With our lack of humility comes pride; trying to make sure everything looks all right for the general body of judgmental individuals that surround us at any given time. We don't reach out for help when we need it. We put on the front that everything is fine, even if it's not. This creates more pride, which creates less humility. Thus, we spend a good part of our time pretending rather than being real and honest about who we are and what is most important to us.

I have met too many ministers over the years who literally drive themselves into all sorts of illnesses, physical maladies, and sometimes even death trying to prove themselves "successful" in some abstract concept of what success is. This has passed on to congregants, all of whom already struggle with their concepts of success. Every single one of us experienced the disappointment of someone we knew or loved earlier in our lives who felt what we did or wanted to do wasn't right or wasn't good enough. We desired to become successful to either satisfy them or topple their concepts of success. Somewhere in here, we all learned that we need to measure up to an outside, abstract idea of what it means to be successful, and we started pursuing that, even if we are Christian.

As believers, we need to take a deep breath, a moment of *selah* pause, and consider what we deem success in this life through the view of humility. God can't work through someone who is so busy pursuing their own agenda and own ideas about what they want to do (no matter how altruistic those things may seem) that they can't step back and allow Him pause and purpose in his or her life. Talking about humility is more than just a nice ideal for our work and our purpose in this Christian life: it's the very fundamental foundation by which God can interact with us and move through us by the Spirit and with His grace in our lives.

Learning humility isn't easy, but it is necessary. Let us talk about our decrease, and His increase, because our spiritual lives depend upon it.

ARE WE SUPPOSED TO BE HUMBLE...OR NOT?

If you think about the messages we receive in church, they are, overall, often confusing. For example, we are told that "we're the head and not the tail," but then we are told to remain humble. We're told we need to be bold, but then we are told that we need to be cautious. We're told that we can do anything, but then we are told to make sure that all we do remains within God's will. We're told to be successful, but then we are told to make sure we don't get "too successful." We're told that we shouldn't be greedy, but then we are encouraged to aspire for things we don't need, such as bigger houses and cars. Then we are told we should do for or share with others, but as a church we are never given the opportunity to do so or told just how we should go about doing that. These few examples are just a small sample of the contradictory messages we receive from the pulpit.

If you have ever been a part of a message or a series of messages and found yourself rather lost because the one message seemed to contradict itself or it contradicted another message previously taught, you are not alone. It's unfortunate we feel the need to cheerlead every message we hear, but a discerning heart goes a long way in our honesty with God, ourselves, and others in the Kingdom. If there's something you're not understanding, questions must be asked. Odds are good that whoever delivered the message has never thought about its contradicting or conflicting nature before, and this is because nobody ever has called them on it.

People aren't called to accountability for their teachings for many reasons. One of the main ones drives home at the need for "success" we just spoke of earlier. Being successful in a worldly (or popular) sense has removed the focus from quality ministry and put it instead on how well-received what one says may be. Couple this with an overall poorly educated clergy (individuals who receive credentials without training) and we have a total mess on our hands. People gravitate toward that which is most entertaining rather than that which is clear and understandable, and we have the result we see, now. Most ministers take their lead from popular Christian preachers, authors, and almost stardom-esque people who teach without proper understanding, do not have proper clergy credentials, and are, honestly, giving us the wrong ideas about Christianity and the Christian lifestyle.

Not too long ago, I was on Facebook and approached via inbox by a minister from overseas. He asked me, "How can pastors grow their churches?" I thought about the question before I answered it. I told him that, quite frankly, I don't like questions like this one. It is my belief that every pastor's situation is different and there is no such thing as "twelve ways to grow your church." I also stated that it's not my purpose in ministry to teach people how to be popular, but how to do things properly. He didn't really answer me, because the response wasn't what he expected. This conversation, however, was very eye-opening to me about many of the struggles I've had as a minister over the years. In my ministry, I've worked very hard not to give contradictory messages. That means those who are a part of it or follow it must humble themselves to receive what is taught. Here, we change. This isn't a place where we get together and puff everyone up to the ceiling, but a place where we all empty ourselves so God can fill us up. That's hard for many to receive, and the evidence of that is the mess we often talk about the church having within its ranks. Yet, for a mess that is so commonly acknowledged, I don't hear much about how to correct that mess. We might complain and whine, but the reason we don't hear how to resolve it is because resolving the mess requires us – all of us – ministers as well as laity – to humble ourselves before the face of God and stop seeking after things that deliberately confuse and confound us.

At that time Solomon and all Israel celebrated the Festival of Booths. A very large crowd had come from the territory between the border of Hamath and the River of Egypt. On the eighth day there was an assembly. They had observed the dedication of the altar for seven days and celebrated the festival for another seven days. On the twenty-third day of the seventh month, Solomon dismissed the people to their tents. They rejoiced with cheerful hearts for all the blessings the Lord had given David, Solomon, and His people Israel.

Solomon finished the Lord's temple and the royal palace and completed everything he had in mind for the Lord's temple and his own palace. Then the Lord appeared to him at night. He said to Solomon,

"I have heard your prayer
    and have chosen this place for Myself as a temple for sacrifices.
I may shut the sky so that there is no rain,
    or command grasshoppers to devour the countryside,
    or send an epidemic among My people.
However, if My people, who are called by My Name,
    will humble themselves,
    pray, search for Me, and turn from their evil ways,
        then I will hear their prayer from heaven, forgive their sins,
    and heal their country.
        My eyes will be open,
            and My ears will pay attention to those prayers at this place. (2 Chronicles 7:8-15)

We love to quote 2 Chronicles 7:14 around political holidays or when things are out of control in a nation, but have we ever listened to its words or context? These words were spoken after the completion of the temple and after Israel finished the celebration of the Festival of Booths. The people of Israel were in good spirits, happy and excited about the place of their nation. Solomon prayed and then God appeared to him by night with this message. He was letting Solomon know how to handle catastrophes that might come (specifically epidemic or natural disaster). We know how such times are – they are confusing. They bring with them people who confuse us. They try to teach us things that make sense of what's going on and make sense of the situations, but they aren't words that herald from God and lead the proper way, because they leave out key elements in being divinely directed. The Scriptures clearly tell us the answer out of confusion is to humble ourselves, pray, seek God, and turn away from the evil that we do. When we do this, we will find the answers that we seek.

This is a message we need to hear in church: we need to humble ourselves; we need to pray in earnest, seek God, not just as a musing or a figurehead, but as exactly the Father He is to us, and turn away from our evil. Let me underline turn away from our evil, as in the evil each one of us does (whether we want to admit we do it through sin, or not). We must stop looking to everything but God for our answers, and see Him as our source, the source of all, to change and transform us, moving from the uncertain to purposeful and enlightening. This starts when we humble ourselves, recognizing we can't do it all alone. No matter how many positive thinking chants we embrace or mantras we say, we can't do this without God. Humility recognizes this, embraces Him within our walk, and lets Him do for us that which we cannot do on our own.

GOD IS NOT THE AUTHOR OF CONFUSION

Confusion is the result of situations in our lives that are either not of God or out of the will of God. It doesn't mean we are always the ones who are out of God's will or not doing His will, but it can result from others who might be around us or close to us who might be in such a state. If we humble ourselves in honesty, there are many who must admit that living in a state of confusion is a way of life, a complicated state of being that they've been trying to navigate for many years. We've all made bad choices or kept people in our lives past their seasons with us. It can be hard to let people go, especially if they are close family or friends. Sometimes we bring confusion into our lives ourselves, because we avoid obeying what God wants us to do, or we run our own interference with our own needs, pride, or lack of humility.

So what does this mean, brothers and sisters? When you gather, each person has a psalm, doctrine, revelation, another language, or an interpretation. Everything must be done to help each other grow. If people speak in other languages, only two or three at the most should speak. They should do it one at a time, and someone must interpret what each person says. But if an interpreter isn't present, those people should remain silent in church. They should only speak to themselves and to God.

Two or three people should speak what God has revealed. Everyone else should decide whether what each person said is right or wrong. If God reveals something to another person who is seated, the first speaker should be silent. All of you can take your turns speaking what God has revealed. In that way, everyone will learn and be encouraged. People who speak what God has revealed must control themselves. God is not a God of disorder but a God of peace. (1 Corinthians 14:26-33)

1 Corinthians 14 is a long chapter about issues of order in the church, specifically the issue of setting order. It's not an accident this chapter is often misinterpreted. In an ironic turn, many try to use it to maintain their own sense of disorder, because those are most comfortable. Pride, chasing after successes, false teaching, improper ambitions, and error in the church, are all things that create confusion for us. God is not the author of confusion! When you are unable to hear from God or you deal with spiritual interference, you are most likely in a situation where confusion is, in some way, present. That means whenever we are in a situation that spawns chaos, not only are we not being used by God, but we also can't hear from God to be properly used by Him.

The Apostle Paul recognized that people love chaos. The goal of chaos is for someone to rise to the top, in the hopes they will garner the most attention. Everyone loves to do everything with themselves in mind, even with the agenda or purpose of spiritual gifts, even with the things of God…and such must be immediately shut down. In place of chaos, we must find humility: people who are able to respect the gifts of others, allow others to exercise their gifts, being able to be silent when others are speaking, extending common courtesy, and sit still while God reveals whatever it is He desires to reveal. We must be teachable, humble, and in control of ourselves. When we do this, He can increase within us, because our understanding of Him shall be greater, as shall the understanding He provides of our purpose in this life.

Competition

Competition is a word we are never supposed to utter in Christian circles. We think if we pretend it's not there, it doesn't exist. Yet competition lives in the church, alive, well, and thriving. It's the very thing that keeps ministers from supporting each other, churches from spiritual health, and people from reaching out in Christian love to help one another. It's the very thing that drives us to worldly success, the hope to "be somebody" in the eyes of others.

It's also killing our relationship with God, not to mention other people.

Before you immediately say this is not you, you need to think long and hard about your ambitions and why you desire them. Ambition is not, in and of itself, a wrong thing. God has given us dreams and visions. Those dreams and visions do not become reality if we don't have some motivation behind them. It's good to want to do things with your life and to make the most of the years you have while you are here, because we only have so many. Good use of time, seeking goals, achieving things, anticipating good to come from your productivity, these are all good things, important and essential to a purposeful life. The question that edges in with competition, however, is why are you doing it?

We convince ourselves all the time that our motives and goals are altruistic when they are not such in any way, shape, or form. Desiring a large, international ministry sounds really good, doesn't it? Think of all the souls that can be saved, the people who can be helped, and the lives that can be transformed! It sounds sacrificial. It sounds noble. It sounds spiritual. And if you have the wrong motive, it can sound however you want. If the purpose of ministry is to squash everyone else, be famous, be a household name, have a lot of money, or show up someone in our lives who said we can't do it or won't be able to…we are doing ministry to be competitive. It might work for awhile, but eventually…it will stop.

"A priest's lips should preserve knowledge. Then, because he is the messenger for the Lord of Armies, people will seek instruction from his mouth.

"But you have turned from the correct path and caused many to stumble over my teachings. You have corrupted the promise made to Levi," says the Lord of Armies. "So I have made you disgusting, and I have humiliated you in front of all the people, because you have not followed My ways. You have been unfair when applying My teachings." (Malachi 2:7-9)

Malachi's words may seem unpopular, but they reveal intense truths about how seriously God takes deceptive practices. Whether we like to deal with it (or we don't), at some point in time, God shuts down competitions that misrepresent His Name. Whether we compete with others or on some level we compete with the ministries of old, competition has no place in God's work.

The same is true whether we are talking about ministry or anything in life. In our base nature, we measure ourselves against everyone around us and everyone we see, especially against those who seem to be doing better than we are at whatever it is that we do. If we're single, we think there's something wrong with us for not being married, if we're married, our marriage isn't as good as someone else's, if we're an employee, someone else is a better one, if we have our own business, someone else makes more money at it, if we are in church, someone seems more spiritual than us. It's the way of the world, and it dominates way too much of our time, our thoughts, and our being.

The Lord is good and decent.
   That is why He teaches sinners the way they should live.
He leads humble people to do what is right,
   and He teaches them His way.
Every path of the Lord is one of mercy and truth
   for those who cling to His promise and written instructions. (Psalm 25:8-10)

A person's pride will humiliate him,
   but a humble spirit gains honor. (Proverbs 29:23)

God leads the humble. Competitive people are rooted in pride and are unwilling to go where they need to go. Humility strips this exterior competition from us by reducing us to who we are before God, as we are. This might sound strange, but if we are brought before God to deal with and address ourselves, the competitive edge of others loses its vision and focus. It is God's desire that we will step away from focusing so much on how we look next to someone else and discover how we look to God and how we look to ourselves. Humility hushes the noise of everyone and everything around us, the confusion that seeks to infiltrate and destroy, and gives us the grounding to get where we need to be, in truth and honesty.

<u>Help when we need it</u>

Admitting we need help, swallowing our pride, stepping aside from the concerns of what others might think, and stepping up to the plate in humility is a huge step for us when it comes to allowing God to work within us and to bring change in our lives.

If we acknowledge God has created us for relationship, that means some things we just can't do for ourselves. It's a nice concept that we will be self-sufficient in all things, but that completely defies the notion that God is here for us and so are others around us. In humility, we stop seeing others as a competitive edge and God as a fearful judge and start acknowledging our own limitations, weaknesses, and areas where we just can't handle things on our own.

"I am the vine. You are the branches. Those who live in Me while I live in them will produce a lot of fruit. But you can't produce anything without Me. Whoever doesn't live in Me is thrown away like a branch and dries up. Branches like this are gathered, thrown into a fire, and burned. If you live in Me and what I say lives in you, then ask for anything you want, and it will be yours. You give glory to My Father when you produce a lot of fruit and therefore show that you are My disciples...You didn't choose Me, but I chose you. I have appointed you to go, to produce fruit that will last, and to ask the Father in My Name to give you whatever you ask for. Love each other. This is what I'm commanding you to do." (John 15:5-8,16-17)

Our bodies have many parts, but these parts don't all do the same thing. In the same way, even though we are many individuals, Christ makes us one body and individuals who are connected to each other. (Romans 12:4-5)

Help carry each other's burdens. In this way you will follow Christ's teachings. (Galatians 6:2)

We must also consider how to encourage each other to show love and to do good things. We should not stop gathering together with other believers, as some of you are doing. Instead, we must continue to encourage each other even more as we see the day of the Lord coming. (Hebrews 10:24-25)

The Scriptures might not always be clear about some things, but they are explicitly clear about the following: we need God, we need to be connected to God, we need to remain connected to God (through Christ) to continue to produce good things in our lives. We also, like it or not, must be connected to other people. This isn't just about us, it's not about focusing on us, and you'd be amazed at how connected humility is to being able to work well with God and others.

See, here is the thing: we can't do anything in a relationship without humility. Relationships without humility become dictatorships that selfishly cater to someone else's needs or result in constant fights for attention and control. If we are going to be involved with others, we need to know enough of ourselves and enough of God working within us to be humble, not esteeming ourselves less than others but not as superior to them, either. When we do so, we know that an attitude that does not seek its own way is key to spiritual growth in any situation.

No, you can't build a ministry by yourself. No, you can't have a successful marriage by yourself. No, you can't be a great parent by yourself. No, you can't do your job by yourself. Everything in this life requires us to find that balance between being so eager to give to others that we are not usable by God because we get worn out and being so selfish, we never give to anyone. Our prayer needs to be that we connect with those who are right for Kingdom building and that in all things, we will maintain our connection to God, Who leads and guides us on how we can better serve one another, in all humility.

GIFTING ATTRIBUTES OF THE HOLY SPIRIT

Before the New Testament writers mused about spiritual gifts, the book of Isaiah spoke of seven gifting attributes that come forth from the Spirit of God. They are spoken of as emanating from the Spirit of God and resting upon Someone (and, by extension, those who are found to be in that Someone).

Then a shoot will come out from the stump of Jesse,
and a branch from its roots will bear fruit.
The Spirit of the Lord will rest on Him—
the Spirit of wisdom and understanding,
the Spirit of advice and power,
the Spirit of knowledge and fear of the Lord.
He will gladly bear the fear of the Lord.
He will not judge by what His eyes see
or decide by what His ears hear.
He will judge the poor justly.
He will make fair decisions for the humble people on earth.
He will strike the earth with a rod from His mouth.
He will kill the wicked with the breath from His lips.

Justice will be the belt around His waist.
Faithfulness will be the belt around His hips. (Isaiah 11:1-5)

There's no question the Messianic nature of this prophecy points to Jesus Christ. It doesn't just tell us about Jesus, however. It also tells us about the desired character of His followers. The Scriptures do tell us the church shall one day judge the world and rule with Christ, but the problem is when we hear these different verses, we hear them without the humble balance needed to execute proper leadership. Instead of hearing these attributes as a must, as foundational aspects of being built up in the Lord when we have properly humbled ourselves before Him, we hear about being "in charge." I assure you, if you don't exemplify the gifting attributes of the Spirit, you will not be a candidate for leadership! These different attributes are:

- **The Spirit of the Lord:** The Holy Spirit, the very source of all we speak of here in terms of gifting attributes (Isaiah 61:1-3).

- **Wisdom:** A practical application of God's living Word that changes one's life; good judgment, the ability to foresee results, and perspective only God can provide (Proverbs 3:13-24).

- **Understanding:** The ability to empty oneself and personal perspective to allow God to educate them in the truth of a matter; fosters compassion and truth about a situation (Job 32:8-11).

- **Advice (counsel):** The ability to implement wisdom and give advice; provide perspective, counsel, and wisdom (Psalm 73:21-28).

- **Power (strength):** The ability to endure in any situation; endurance, withstanding obstacles, creativity (1 Corinthians 4:20).

- **Knowledge:** Being able to learn, apply learning, and being able to interact through learning; learning, education, the pursuit of learning (Proverbs 18:15-21).

- **Fear (awe) of the Lord:** Fear of the Lord isn't fear in the sense we often think of it. It's not something crippling that causes us to run and hide from God. It is a sense of amazement and reverential awe for God, as one positions themselves in humility next to the incredible Being and power that is God, our Creator; respect, reverence, honor (Proverbs 1:7).

Walking in humility is a powerful thing because it opens the door for us to receive and maintain much more spiritual responsibility in our lives. Isaiah 11:1-5 lists responsibilities, a command and a call to handle things fairly and with equality. Those are characteristics absent from our world, aren't they? All over the world, even in our own country, we hear cries of people who are treated unjustly and unfairly. The reason we do not find proper justice in this world is because we do not follow leadership that echoes the foundational principles of humility. We don't expect enough of our spiritual leaders, nor our natural ones, and in our ambitions for political power or the advance of certain causes, we overlook the character of our leaders for the sake of a different goal. Over time, this catches up with us, as we watch leaders oppress, disdain, and abuse the people they are supposed to lead.

Only when we humble ourselves can we govern anyone – or anything – well. You might not be a leader in church or in a ministry, but there is somewhere or something in your life that requires your governance, and that you can govern better. Right governance starts with your humility as you let God increase within you and increase your perceptions and awareness in each situation, so you are better able to handle everything that comes along.

OBEDIENCE

We spoke a little bit about obedience earlier, but obedience is a key thing as God increases within us and we decrease. Obedience is one of those big words that most Christians despise, and most preachers avoid. We avoid it because we don't understand it. When we get up in the pulpit and harp on it, we are trying to get a point across with it that won't really challenge anyone. The concept of obedience and obeying God often seems abstract to us. In the Scriptures, it seems like God's will was really obvious to people, right? God came down from wherever He is and told them exactly what to do, and there was no question what was going to happen or how it was going to come about. So, what do we do now that God isn't coming down from the sky to give us direction? I mean, didn't that work better than us trying to figure it out for ourselves?

There are a few things we need to consider with this viewpoint, which I know is far from foreign. The first thing is that we really don't know how God spoke to every single person in Biblical times. We know He spoke and delivered a message to them, but we don't always know if they received that message audibly, through the inward witness of the Spirit, in a dream or a vision, through an angelic encounter, or any of the many other possible ways that God speaks to people (which we discussed in the previous chapter). Thinking that it was easier to hear from God in ancient times is a misnomer. People still had their immediate lives, cultures, feelings, and biases to cut through to hear from God. They still had to overcome their own doubts and fears when it came to obedience. Knowing you heard from God in those days was a rare thing. They had the feeling of not being quite certain what it meant then, maybe more so than people do today. The second thing we need to consider is that people still had to discern what was from God from what might have been them. They had to pioneer spiritual obedience in a world that was unfamiliar with that concept.

The third thing, and perhaps the most relevant of them all to consider, is that obedience can be hard, no matter who is obedient or what God asks someone to do. We grow up thinking that one day we will be adults, and we will no longer have to be obedient. We'll be able to chart the course of our own lives and do what we want. That is the promise of childhood: becoming a free adult who doesn't have to be told what to do, whether it's homework, eat vegetables, clean behind our ears, or go to bed at a certain time. Human nature, the part of us that is dominated by the flesh, loves the idea of our independence. We don't want anyone or anything to tell us what we must do or that we should do something, even if it's for our own good. Now that we are adults, that same nature is seldom, if ever satisfied, because adulthood carries with it its own responsibilities and unique obedience. We must do our jobs properly and follow the established rules therein. We must treat our boss with respect, even if we despise them or think they do a subpar job. We deal with deadlines and timelines and endless bills that must be paid on time, or else we will reap far more dire consequences than a childhood grounding or loss of privileges. There are so many things we say we want to do or are going to do, but because we have things we must do out of obedience to life and life's requirements, we don't get around to most of them.

The principle of independence is contrary to our creation for relationship. Yes, we do stand before God by ourselves, but God also takes into account how we got where we are and what connections are involved to create our situations, our faults, and our sins. We don't sin by ourselves. We don't succeed by ourselves. We don't govern, nor do we rule by ourselves. Everything that we do in this life is connected to others, whether we are aware of it, or not. God created us for relationship with Him and with others. Even though it might not seem so obvious, the concept of obedience is related to relationship. It is rooted in a true desire to do our best by others (not to mention do what is often best for ourselves) and to make sure the world in which we live is a safe place for everyone that's in it. See, whenever someone makes a request of us, no matter how old we might be – to stop doing something or to please do something – whenever we answer that request – we are following a principle of obedience.

But oh my, how do we hate having to think about or do what's best for other people. We want it to be all about us! We live in this state of parallel confusion, fighting for our own independent maintenance and our relationships with others. We want relationships, but we typically don't like them very much when they require us to give something of ourselves.

The same is true with our attitude with God. We love to hear about God's promises, all that He wants to do for us, and all the benefits of being in a relationship with Him. I could write a book about the promises of God, and everyone I know would run out to buy it, just because it would appeal to the idea that everything about God goes their way. Yes, it's true, there are benefits to being in relationship with God, but those benefits aren't where a relationship with God begins and ends. Just like any relationship, obedience is a principle that plays an important part in its health and functionality. Blessings are awesome. Promises are great. Obedience is still real though, even though it might not sell out stadiums or create best-selling books.

When it comes to obeying God, I don't think it's a big stretch to assume most people don't like the idea, period. They prefer the concept of God as permissible, quick to forgive our wrongdoings and sins, overlooking our proclivities to stubbornness and disobedience. We want to hear what God is going to do for us, not what He might ask of us. Obedience, however, is a central aspect of our relationship with God, because it is one of the ways that we learn His will. It is that place between aligning with God's will and not always understanding that will for ourselves while we are in this life. We might not recognize the reason why God has us do things, but in obedience, we trust Him enough to do whatever it is He is leading us to do.

Then the Lord spoke to Samuel: "I regret that I made Saul king. He turned away from me and did not carry out My instructions." Samuel was angry, and he prayed to the Lord all night. Early in the morning he got up to meet Saul. Samuel was told, "Saul went to Carmel to set up a monument in his honor. Then he left there and went to Gilgal."

Samuel came to Saul, who said, "The Lord bless you. I carried out the Lord's instructions."

However, Samuel asked,

"But what is this sound of sheep in my ears
 and this sound of cows that I hear?"

Saul answered, "The army brought them from the Amalekites. They spared the best sheep and cows to sacrifice to the Lord your God. But the rest they claimed for God and destroyed."

"Be quiet," Samuel told Saul, "and let me tell you what the Lord told me last night."

"Speak," Saul replied.

Samuel said, "Even though you don't consider yourself great, you were the head of Israel's tribes. The Lord anointed you king of Israel. And the Lord sent you on a mission. He said, 'Claim those sinners, the Amalekites, for me by destroying them. Wage war against them until they're wiped out.' Why didn't you obey the Lord? Why have you taken their belongings and done what the Lord considers evil?"

"But I did obey the Lord," Saul told Samuel. "I went where the Lord sent me, brought back King Agag of Amalek, and claimed the Amalekites for God. The army took some of their belongings—the best sheep and cows were claimed for God—in order to sacrifice to the Lord your God in Gilgal."

Then Samuel said,
"Is the Lord as delighted with burnt offerings and sacrifices
 as he would be with your obedience?
To follow instructions is better than to sacrifice.
To obey is better than sacrificing the fat of rams.
 The sin of black magic is rebellion.
 Wickedness and idolatry are arrogance.

Because you rejected the Lord's word,
He rejects you as king."

Then Saul told Samuel, "I have sinned by not following the Lord's command or your instructions. I was afraid of the people and listened to them. Now please forgive my sin and come back with me so that I may worship the Lord."
Samuel told Saul, "I will not go back with you because you rejected what the Lord told you. So the Lord rejects you as king of Israel." When Samuel turned to leave, Saul grabbed the hem of his robe, and it tore. Samuel told him, "The Lord has torn the kingdom of Israel from you today. He has given it to your neighbor who is better than you. In addition, the Glory of Israel does not lie or change his mind, because he is not a mortal who changes his mind."

Saul replied, "I have sinned! Now please honor me in front of the leaders of my people and in front of Israel. Come back with me, and let me worship the Lord your God." Then Samuel turned and followed Saul, and Saul worshiped the Lord.

"Bring me King Agag of Amalek," Samuel said.

Agag came to him trembling. "Surely, the bitterness of death is past," Agag said.

But Samuel said, "As your sword made women childless, so your mother will be made childless among women." And Samuel cut Agag in pieces in the presence of the Lord at Gilgal.

Then Samuel went to Ramah, and Saul went to his home at Gibeah. Samuel didn't see Saul again before he died, though Samuel mourned over Saul. And the Lord regretted that he had made Saul king of Israel. (1 Samuel 15:10-35)

The story of Saul's rulership over Israel is summarized here through the fruit of Saul's work. He stood out, so disobedient before God and ignoring God's words, unto seeking a medium for himself. However, God's disdain for Saul's leadership started before Saul ever became king. Saul was the product of a rebellious people who wanted to disobey God and fit in with their neighbors, looking like and behaving like every other nation that was around them. They didn't want to have to obey God directly. The people asked for a king, and a king they got: Saul, who might have looked the part and appeared to be the part, but who was completely ill equipped and maligned for leadership over the nation of Israel.

Saul just wanted to say he was sorry for doing the wrong things and return to everything as normal, so he could be comfortable and maintain his leadership. Yet even though we know we serve a forgiving God, the Lord wasn't quite so understanding with Saul's apology. God knew Saul wasn't really sorry for what he did. His apology was designed to restore himself in the eyes of the people, with God's support. In other words, Saul wanted to maintain his independence. He wanted to do things his own way but still wanted to have God's favor at the same time.

Sounds like anyone you might know?

The word to Saul was simple: It's better to be obedient than to offer sacrifice. In other words, it's better to do what we know is right from the beginning rather than doing the wrong thing and having to atone for it. When we know God has called us to do something, it's better to do it as opposed to having to make up for not doing it later. So much of our lives are caught up in Saul-like pursuits: looking the part, wanting to be like everyone else, trying to do it our own way, and then winding up in a situation where we must repent, because we didn't do what would honor God from the very beginning.

Our walk with God is full of enough sacrifices to the flesh and difficult places as we grow and transform, rather than deliberately being in situations that will require sacrifice to try and make something right because we disobeyed God. Obedience is a place of trust, where we are willing to take God at His Word and believe His promises are real, even if we don't see and understand it all in this realm, just yet.

SACRIFICE

Sacrifice is one of those topics that make most Christians decidedly uncomfortable. In discussing sacrifice here in this chapter, we aren't talking about sacrifice for our sins or the concept that we are going to work our salvation. That work was done for us by Jesus Himself. No amount of sacrifice, giving things up, or attempting to do different things to get noticed by God will save you. The kind of sacrifice we are talking about is the type that helps us grow. It comes along with walking through the Christian life and following the call of God as it arises. I should clarify that it's a part of everyone's life; it is just the Christian who is able to plug into God and make sense of that sacrificial discomfort. On the surface, sacrifice just seems like something unpleasant that we must go through. Odds are good, there's part of us that feels we won't make it through. In the long run, learning how to make sacrifice – and make it well – rests in the humble hearts of those who are ready for a change.

Sacrifice is the precept of giving up one thing for something else. In salvation, Christ gave Himself up in our place, for our sins. In the Old Testament, various items were offered in place of ourselves for our sins, as types of Christ Who was to come. The principle of sacrifice doesn't end with salvation, though. It might be easy to look over salvation and think we will never have to make another sacrifice again, but such is impractical. The reason for this is simple: the Christian life is a sacrifice, in and of itself. By choosing to be a Christian (and yes, it is a choice), we sacrifice the world, we are willing to sacrifice the flesh, and we are willing to sacrifice our comforts to come to a place of understanding and relationship with God our Father.

An example can be paralleled in everyday life. To be married, you must sacrifice being single. Most single people jump up and down with enthusiasm at such a suggestion. No more lonely, empty beds! No more dating! No more showing up for events as a single person! Sex anytime you want it! Financial help with the bills! Help with household responsibilities! Come on, let's trade in the single life! It sounds great; it sounds hopeful, like a new start. Most married people, however, will tell you that as much as there might be things they don't miss about single life, there are things that are hard to give up and easy to miss. The freedom to go where you want without question, having to discuss matters with another person, having to include someone else in financial decisions, having to communicate well when all you want to do is shut down somewhere, negotiations with chores, sorting through sexual preferences, and the realization that you aren't just living for yourself anymore – all require sacrifice. They require giving up and trading in your little black book, going out night after night to the club or the parties, and doing things your own way. It might not sound like a hard trade-off, but when it comes down to it, giving up of ourselves is always hard. We might make relationships of all sorts desirable and sound like they are worth it, but they require sacrifice on our part. When marriage doesn't go as expected and neither party sacrifices the way they should, marriages experience difficulties.

We like to think of relationships as some sort of divine answer to cure loneliness. While it's certainly true that eliminating loneliness is a perk of relationships (at least in most cases), God's purpose for all relationships is different than just curing what ails us in terms of our emotional voids. Relationships drive home with principles of holiness and sacrifice, which require us to grow as people. It's during the times we stretch as people and gain deeper insight into the call to love as God loves and understand through humility placed within all of us.

The slogan, "It's just me and Jesus!" is reflected on television, social media, and even in many churches. It's catchy and makes people think their spiritual interactions will be controlled and easy. This sounds like the perfect, sacrifice-less life. It's also a total lie. As we go through our lives, God deliberately places us in situations that demand we make choices to grow as spiritual beings, as people who transform their image as they put on the mind of Christ. This comes about as we sacrifice – as He increases, and we decrease.

Then Jesus said to His disciples, "Those who want to come with me must say no to the things they want, pick up their crosses, and follow Me. Those who want to save their lives will lose them. But those who lose their lives for Me will find them." (Matthew 16:24-25)

Those who want to save their lives will lose them. But those who lose their lives for Me will save them. (Luke 9:24)

Then Peter said, "We've left everything to follow You."

Jesus said to them, "I can guarantee this truth: Anyone who gave up his home, wife, brothers, parents, or children because of God's Kingdom will certainly receive many times as much in this life and will receive eternal life in the world to come." (Luke 18:28-30)

To gain something, we must give something up. That's the principle of sacrifice. To follow Christ, we must give up the grip we hold over controlling our lives as independent agents. To discover God's will, we must give up thinking we are more than we are and embrace Who He is. We must sacrifice, over and over again, so we can receive the fullness God has for us.

LEARNING

Have you ever met someone in an arranged marriage? If you have, you probably had lots of questions about the foundation of their relationship. You probably wondered, as most do, about the dynamics where two literal strangers go from meeting once or twice (if that much) to being married, living in the same home, and expected to share the intimacies of life together. From the stories I have read, most arranged marriages are awkward, particularly at first. The adjustment of not just having to know your new extended family, but also your spouse, creates very difficult and trying situations. The feelings of love and infatuation present in early relationships are usually not there. Instead, almost every story relates is the need to get to know one another. Over time, they come to know their mate because they discipline themselves to know one another. Some stories end with expressions of love that develop over time and some do not, but the consistent aspect of the story is their need to learn their mate. They make a point to know one another because they are now married. Whether they like it or not, they have to learn how to live with one another and adjust to married life.

Sometimes I think we take the concept of relationship for granted because we are used to relying on our feelings and emotional states as guides for how we behave and interact with others. We think butterflies in the stomach and a desire to spend all our time with someone are what make a relationship suitable for marriage. One thing we can learn from people who have been in arranged marriages is whether feelings or not, nothing is a substitute for the true discipline needed in learning about one another. This doesn't stop because we are attracted to someone or because someone seems to be a desirable mate. No matter how long someone is in a marriage, there are always things they can learn about their mate.

The same is true in our relationship with God. We don't get saved, have a rush of emotions, and are suddenly done learning about God. If we approach our relationship with God like this, we'll miss out on the expanse of Who He is. Throughout our lives, we must continue to learn about God by loving those things which He has created and learning about those things, as they tell us about Him.

The wise also will hear and increase in learning, and the person of understanding will acquire skill and attain to sound counsel [so that he may be able to steer his course rightly]—

That people may understand a proverb and a figure of speech or an enigma with its interpretation, and the words of the wise and their dark sayings or riddles. (Proverbs 1:5-6, AMPC)

The wise in heart are called prudent, understanding, and knowing, and winsome speech increases learning [in both speaker and listener].

Understanding is a wellspring of life to those who have it, but to give instruction to fools is folly.

The mind of the wise instructs his mouth, and adds learning and persuasiveness to his lips. (Proverbs 16:21-23, AMPC)

There is much to learn in this life that will help us recognize God's wisdom and insight into situations we will face. Learning does not just inspire us to do better and be smarter, however. We should never, ever tire of learning, because through learning, we draw close to God. Learning inspires a whole new sense of love and knowledge of God in a way nothing else can offer us. It is certainly true that we draw near to the Lord through things such as prayer, worship, and time spent with God, but these aren't the only ways that we come to know Him in relationship. When we learn, we expand our minds and realize that God is far bigger and grander than anything we can imagine.

GIVING

Giving is a basic Biblical principle. God has given to us abundantly from the fullness of all that He is. He has given to us through creation, through the work of Christ in salvation, and He continues to give and provide for us, every day, and in every way. Most only think about giving when it comes to money (offerings, tithes, gifts), but giving a gift can come in any form, whether financial, material, spiritual, or emotional. Giving is important because whenever we give, we are humbling ourselves to give a part of ourselves to God or to another person.

Give, and you will receive. A large quantity, pressed together, shaken down, and running over will be put into your pocket. The standards you use for others will be applied to you. (Luke 6:38)

If we are Christians, we are required to give. We should always be giving of ourselves, our time, out of all God has given to us in this life, and from our finances. We should also be people who give in the form of volunteering, reaching out to help others, offer kind and encouraging words, and make sure that we are people who know that giving is more than handing off money in every circumstance.

From a young age, children should be taught to give, both to the church and to others. As adults, we should make sure giving is a priority, something we make a focal point in our lives. It is something we can all do, young or old, rich or poor, regardless of gender it in our minds that all we have to do is give to others through money. We should also be people who reach out when people are hurting, volunteer our time and do things for others without cost, offer kind words, and ensure that we make sure we know how to give more than just our money.

As Jesus sat facing the temple offering box, He watched how much money people put into it. Many rich people put in large amounts. A poor widow dropped in two small coins, worth less than a cent.

He called his disciples and said to them, "I can guarantee this truth: This poor widow has given more than all the others. All of them have given what they could spare. But she, in her poverty, has given everything she had to live on." (Mark 12:41-44)

The poor widow's story is about more than just giving through money. By doing as she did, she teaches us about giving; the importance of giving to God and being someone willing and ready to give. It's not just about giving when we have the money to do so or it's convenient, and it's not just about giving because we think we will get something back for it. Too often we think we can't give because we don't have as much money as somebody else does or we don't have the time or anything useful to give. This is a mistake. It's also a way to circumvent God's principles, thinking they don't apply to us. If we claim to not have, we think we don't have to do what God requires of us. God doesn't just ask for our money; He asks for us. When we give, we do so freely, without expecting to get something back. Giving financially is an expression of how willing we are to give. If we are willing to give our money, we can learn basic principles of giving that extend to other areas of our lives.

None of us like parting with our money; none of us like parting with our time. The reason we don't like doing either is because none of us like parting with ourselves. We want to do what we want to do and giving hits home at our struggle for independence versus relationship. We can't give if we aren't willing to sacrifice part of ourselves for the sake of someone or something else, and if we don't give, we cannot be successful in any of the relationships we have.

God calls us to give because He gives. If we are serious about loving as He loves, we, too, must give.

MODESTY

How would you feel to discover that Scriptural modesty has nothing to do with how long or short someone's skirt is? It shocked me, too. Biblical modesty has nothing to do with the fit of our clothes, but everything to do with something else: money. Biblical modesty is all about being humble enough to recognize everyone doesn't always have what we do, and respecting and loving others enough to refrain from flaunting wealth and income through the way we dress, carry ourselves, and interact with others.

It's not a big secret to realize that a great amount of who we are as people is tied up in how much money we have or how much money others think that we have. We learned it as kids: the one who has the most toys, the best sneakers, the best parties, is the one who "wins." The kids who had the best material things were the ones that everyone wanted to be around, hang out with, be seen with, and imitate. They might have even gotten special treatment from those in authority in school (and sometimes at church): dodging late assignments, avoiding punishment, and being treated as if they are better than others, especially those who were poor.

Following into our teen years and now later as adults, a certain sense of shame accompanies when we don't have the income or material things that others have. We learned this because of how we were treated as children when someone had more and we had less, or we had more, and they had less (as we discussed in the last paragraph). Maybe we were teased for wearing our older sibling's clothes or were mocked for not having the latest, best toys. On the inverse, maybe we were the ones who teased someone else for what they had or didn't have. Whatever our experience was, we learned that having less was something to be ashamed of, and having more was better. We got the clear message that if we don't have money, and all that money brings with it, we should feel bad about ourselves.

We can easily grow depressed and have a negative self-image if we don't have the kind of money we desire or think we should have. Whenever we feel badly about ourselves, we always want to…you guessed right…spend money. We think we "deserve" whatever we want to buy and think spending money is the answer to all the issues we face. We tie our self-worth to our money and our spending, and the result is an entire world full of industries designed to illicit self-esteem through spending.

What does all this have to do with modesty? Everything.

I want women to show their beauty by dressing in appropriate clothes that are modest and respectable. Their beauty will be shown by what they do, not by their hair styles or the gold jewelry, pearls, or expensive clothes they wear. (1 Timothy 2:9)

This passage specifically mentions women, but it applies to all believers. Women are the ones mentioned here because in ancient society, women made sure to attire themselves to display their wealth. The passage isn't condemning wearing jewelry, pearls, or nice clothing. It's fine to be someone who wants to wear something that has meaning or fashionable sense, and who enjoys the world of fashion. (We could also argue the advance of costume jewelry means jewelry is a fashion statement more than one of wealth in modern times, but that is a secondary point.) The passage is condemning the reason why the women were wearing these things. They were wearing such decadence to show off their financial status, to make sure everyone around them knew who they were and how much money they had, even at church. In the church, which was a mixed society of poor and wealthy, flaunting status hit home at the very identity that poisoned culture and created class distinctions. Such was not to exist in the church, because in the church, economic status wasn't of consequence. Everyone present had something to give, and everyone who received it needed something that was supplied.

Modesty is an extension of humility. It reflects how much we buy into exterior ideas about ourselves and the way others perceive us. Are we getting our self-worth and value from the world and then bringing it into church with us, or are we self-valuing because of who we are in Christ? Are we Christian, or conceited? The reflection is in how we carry ourselves, why we wear what we wear, and why we do what we desire to do.

Akin to identity in modesty is identity in worship. If we are constantly about keeping up with others, such creates distraction from spiritual things. These distractions aren't just manifest in our own pursuits, but in the way that we distract others from what really matters. While it's perfectly fine to engage others through likes and interests, we should never allow ourselves to serve as a distraction due to immodesty.

The world will puff us up and conceit us off vanities that pass away. The only anecdote for conceit is humility. We are commanded to embrace modesty because it echoes who we are when we take off all the things the world deems relevant and important. If we can't have all those toys and all those identities the world tells us we need, who are we, at the end of the day?

God wants us to answer. If we can't show through who He is as He works within us, how can we ever be usable by Him?

FORGIVENESS IS MORE THAN A NICE IDEA

Forgiveness. It's a word that either fills you with warm fuzzies, is a theological musing, or is something you'd rather we not discuss all together. Reality says it is probably all three at some point or another. We feel differently about forgiveness, depending on what end of it we find ourselves driven to experience. The realization of being forgiven by God may give us a sense of comfort and freedom. Handling forgiveness with others may not give us quite that same sense of security. Having to ask for forgiveness, give forgiveness, or have someone refuse to forgive you for something doesn't feel really good. Humbling yourself to the point of realizing and admitting you've done something wrong and sinned against someone else doesn't feel really good. Despite how it feels, we must be willing to not just receive forgiveness but offer it and request it when we need it, if we want to be people who have usable hearts.

The current trend is to offer an apology. We say, "I'm sorry," and expect that to be enough, as the world goes on and things continue forward. The problem with "I'm sorry" is that it is overused, and it is not used in a context that has any meaning anymore. When you've hurt someone else, you don't get to decide that you didn't. You don't get to decide that what's happened is now gone because you threw an "I'm sorry" out there, with nothing else attached to it. The same is true if someone has hurt you and just tries to get by without really working to change or transform, themselves. This doesn't reflect true forgiveness, it reflects laziness. It's the hope that we can get by without really employing the true principles of forgiveness in our lives. "I'm sorry" isn't enough. Forgiveness is what's needed. Instead of trying to offer apologies, we need to receive and offer forgiveness.

Several years ago, a woman came to me for ministerial covering. She was so taken with me, she literally attached herself to me. I couldn't go on social media and was afraid to answer my phone because it seemed like she wanted all my attention. She was exhausting to deal with and frustrating to handle. Her countenance was fine when she was with me (or so it would seem), but she seemed to clash with everyone else around us. She was judgmental and critical and had a way of making her bossy attitude seem like spiritual purity and holiness. It didn't take long for her to come to blows with a group of other women I was working with at the time. Her response was to force me to pick either her, who she saw as virtuous, or everyone else, who she saw as negative for me and my ministry work.

I didn't give in to her pressures. She was released, somewhere between two to three months after coming under the ministry. I didn't give her what she desired for a few reasons. The first was that it wasn't right to ask me to throw over everyone else I'd known and worked with much longer than she. The second was because I could see the handwriting on the wall: if I didn't handle her now, she would run me, and this work, ragged. It would become her vision instead of the one that God gave to me, and in doing so, I would lose my standing as the leader He called me to be. Third, her demands were decidedly out of order. I recognize that sometimes we see things in others and want to caution leadership about them, but this wasn't one of those times. This was someone whose goal was to isolate me from everyone else for her own selfish purposes. She wasn't concerned about me, but only about herself.

Her response was less than understanding. She resorted to an all-out attack on social media. The crisis passed, affecting those I knew more than me, because as far as attacks went, it wasn't that intense. She was removed from everything and deleted and blocked, but that didn't stop her. Over a year later, I received an inbox message from her on a social media fan page that was a vile, viscous attack. She followed it up with commentary on a posting on the page. At the time I received the message, I wasn't in a place to deal with her, which, in hindsight, I recognize to be God at work. I was scheduled to speak at a disaster conference, and we were right in the middle of it when she started. I couldn't retort. Instead, after the event was over, I simply blocked her from that page and assumed I'd never hear from her again.

Right after I started writing this book, I heard from this woman again, this time from a new page. Her message was long, telling me where she was now, with a brief message of "apology" for what she had done. In other words, for all her hassling, cyber bullying, harassing messages, and public threats and tantrums, she was offering an "apology." Nothing in her message mentioned a request for forgiveness. She just went on to say where she was, and she'd forwarded something I did six years ago to someone in the church where she was now working.

When I first got the message, I wasn't sure of what to make of it. Something in me didn't want to respond to her. I took the matter in prayer and also took it to some trusted counsel, all of whom agreed that opening up this relationship wasn't a good idea. Then I went and looked at her social media page and noted that even though it had been such a long time, her countenance was exactly the same. She was still trying to lord authority over people without the right to do so, and she was still catty and nasty, backbiting and posting in her style that sounded "holy," but was nothing more than self-seeking and mean. I could see that, apology or not, she was exactly who she was before.

Like I often say, some of us never learn.

The more I prayed about it, the more I gained insight into the difference between apologies and genuine forgiveness. My encounter with this woman was one where I had already worked genuine forgiveness toward her, but not because she'd asked for it or had handled matters correctly. I did it because I needed to move on. Holding on to hostility and resentment toward her wasn't going to change things, not in the least. The situation was over and done with her, but it was not ever made right in the natural realm. There's a difference between a situation being passed and it truly being rectified. Her contact with me wasn't to rectify things, it was to try and start her mess, all over again.

The difference between forgiveness and "I'm sorry" is rectification. We can forgive some, but we don't see rectification. That means forgiveness has not done transforming work in both individuals. Others are so quick to cut people off rather than admitting they've done something wrong, and even when people do recognize wrongdoing, they aren't real quick to ask for forgiveness. Why? If we genuinely practice forgiveness, it demands that we don't just apologize…it demands we do the right thing and make matters right.

So if you are offering your gift at the altar and remember there that another believer has something against you, leave your gift at the altar. First go away and make peace with that person. Then come back and offer your gift. (Matthew 5:23-24)

Then Peter came to Jesus and asked Him, "Lord, how often do I have to forgive a believer who wrongs me? Seven times?"

Jesus answered him, "I tell you, not just seven times, but seventy times seven.

"That is why the Kingdom of heaven is like a king who wanted to settle accounts with his servants. When he began to do this, a servant who owed him millions of dollars was brought to him. Because he could not pay off the debt, the master ordered him, his wife, his children, and all that he had to be sold to pay off the account. Then the servant fell at his master's feet and said, 'Be patient with me, and I will repay everything!'

"The master felt sorry for his servant, freed him, and canceled his debt. But when that servant went away, he found a servant who owed him hundreds of dollars. He grabbed the servant he found and began to choke him. 'Pay what you owe!' he said.

"Then that other servant fell at his feet and begged him, 'Be patient with me, and I will repay you.' But he refused. Instead, he turned away and had that servant put into prison until he would repay what he owed.

"The other servants who worked with him saw what had happened and felt very sad. They told their master the whole story.

"Then his master sent for him and said to him, 'You evil servant! I canceled your entire debt, because you begged me. Shouldn't you have treated the other servant as mercifully as I treated you?'

"His master was so angry that he handed him over to the torturers until he would repay everything that he owed. That is what my Father in heaven will do to you if each of you does not sincerely forgive other believers." (Matthew 18:21-34)

We forgive and are forgiven. We get ourselves right with God. We make things right instead of just leaving them to hang. We make our relationships count, no matter who they might be with. We don't dare approach God if we haven't done the right thing with others, and we are consciously aware of such, because God has placed it on our hearts. When people come in earnest forgiveness to make things right, we forgive. If they never do this, we still forgive. We let God work forgiveness within us, because without forgiveness, there is no Christian message.

A LESSON FROM MOSES' LIFE

Bible characters tend to stand out as larger-than-life in our memories. We think they were great individuals who had loud personalities, led everyone rightly, and never made any mistakes. We don't think of them as being quiet or subdued or ever coming down from their leadership positions.

We're quick to associate leadership with competency and believe that every leader must be up for the job, ready to tackle everything that comes along. If we really look at Bible leaders, however, they don't always quite measure up to the impressions we might have had of them. While our books depict them as strong and bold, it's amazing to note how many of them were downright timid.

Just like modern-day leaders, Bible leaders also represent a diversity of personality types, interests, and levels of extroversion or introversion. There wasn't only one type of leader who rose up to handle the needs of God's people in Bible times. And, just like back then, sometimes Bible leaders don't easily fit with our stereotypes of what a "leader" should be.

Moses was one such Bible character who wasn't the man anyone would have figured as a candidate for leadership. He was quiet, he had a speech impediment, and he honestly didn't want the job. Even when he had the job, he probably had days when he wished someone else could take over the work for him. He came against opposition from the Israelites and even his own relatives. Seeing the face of God and talking directly to God was a big responsibility, especially in the face of such defiance and disobedience among those he led. Despite how he might have felt about the job, Moses was qualified to lead God's people because of one very important fact.

Miriam and Aaron began to criticize Moses because he was married to a woman from Sudan. They asked, "Did the Lord speak only through Moses? Didn't He also speak through us?" The Lord heard their complaint.

(Moses was a very humble man, more humble than anyone else on earth.)

Suddenly, the Lord said to Moses, Aaron, and Miriam, "All three of you come to the tent of meeting." So all three of them came. Then the Lord came down in the column of smoke and stood at the entrance to the tent. He called to Aaron and Miriam, and they both came forward.

He said, "Listen to My words: When there are prophets of the Lord among you, I make Myself known to them in visions or speak to them in dreams. But this is not the way I treat My servant Moses. He is the most faithful person in My household. I speak with him face to face, plainly and not in riddles. He even sees the form of the Lord. Why weren't you afraid to criticize My servant Moses?"

The Lord was angry with them, so He left.

When the smoke left the tent, Miriam was covered with an infectious skin disease. She was as white as snow. Aaron turned to her and saw she was covered with the disease. So he said to Moses, "Please, sir, don't punish us for this foolish sin we committed. Don't let her be like a stillborn baby that's not completely developed."

So Moses cried to the Lord, "Please, God, heal her!"

The Lord replied to Moses, "If her own father had spit in her face, wouldn't she be excluded from the community for seven days? She must be put in isolation outside the camp for seven days. Then she can be brought back." So Miriam was put in isolation outside the camp for seven days. The people didn't break camp until she was brought back. (Numbers 12:1-15)

There aren't too many men who would be so apt to request healing for a sister in this situation. I can vouch I've had times when I was angry with my relatives for less than Miram did, and I still didn't want to pray for anything beneficial for them. She questioned his authority and challenged her own position among the people. According to Bible history, why they opposed Moses' wife varies. Some suggest it is because she was from Sudan (thus outside the Hebrew community); others suggest she was an idolater, and still others say it might have had something to do with racial issues. I think the bigger issue, however, was that they were also angry because Moses had a relationship with God that they didn't understand. They heard from God, interacted prophetically on behalf of God, assisted in the leadership of the Israelite people, and they even spoke for God, so why was Moses always so special? Why did he have special prestige that went along with being "the leader" when they were all involved in the leadership process?

The Scriptures tell us why: Moses was humble. His humility is what separated him from his siblings, as is evident in this passage. While they were busy judging his wife, work, and his relationship and status with God, Moses was doing God's work. He then was the one who interceded for Miriam's healing after the fact. He didn't let what he did interfere with who he was and with his basic relationship and posture before God. Moses knew that in the presence of God, God was to increase, and he was to decrease.

It's difficult to do, and in some ways, hard for us to understand, but it's the only way to go about the spiritual life. If we want God to do incredible things through us, we must step back and be honest with both God and ourselves. The things we often fuss about, stubbornly holding onto them with both hands, are often the things that are the biggest diversions from where we should be in this life. We can't do great things with God if we continue to increase demands, complaints, distractions, and negative behavior. Doing great things with God requires a decrease in everything that keeps us from Him – and an increase in Him and His attributes throughout our days.

There's freedom in letting God do a work within us. Never let your flesh get in the way, because the result of such is the situation that results in alienation, like we saw in Miriam. Even though you might not get a literal skin disease, you may have to spend time away from others to think about your spiritual state with God and where He would have you to be. If we aren't willing to humble ourselves, God will bring circumstances that do it for us. Don't wait, don't linger. Step up to the plate and embrace your own humility in life, allowing Him to increase within you.

(6)
LETTING GOD LEAD YOU

It's clear that you are Christ's letter, written as a result
of our ministry. You are a letter written not with ink
but with the Spirit of the living God, a letter written not
on tablets of stone but on tablets of human hearts.
(2 Corinthians 3:3)

The prophets, visionaries, and mystics of old spoke on the guidance of God in an assortment of ways. It was often difficult for them to describe, because they knew the way they experienced God was not the way the everyday average churchgoer might experience Him. While they had strong experiences that included hearing from God or perceiving Him by the various senses, others might not have ever heard from God in that same way. Most people don't have regular encounters with God...at least not those that are so easily discernable. The work of trying to convert such experiences into practical, relatable language goes to theologians, apostles, pastors, and teachers, who may not know how to explain it well themselves.

Being led by God often seems like a mysterious process to most people, but it doesn't have to be all super-spiritual and deep. God doesn't just lead mystics, prophets, church leaders, or those with a grand and great spiritual story to tell. He leads all of us, often in ways we miss or fail to consider. Because we don't watch how He leads us, we sometimes miss God in our lives in a bigger sense of purpose and meaning.

If we want to be used by God, we must be led by Him. We must know the unique and specific ways He reaches out to us, because it is those different ways that lead us to a greater purpose with Him and purpose within ourselves. Whenever we step back and receive the direction of God, it proves His place in our lives and shows us a whole angle of our relationship that we don't often consider with God. If we believe we are in relationship with God, that means He is involved with us for more than just an hour or two on Sunday mornings and an hour or so during Wednesday Bible study. Being led by God proves and promises that God is a part of us and we of Him, beyond what might seem textbook or comfortable. God is there when we are uncomfortable, when we'd rather He isn't around, and even when we might not assume what we are doing to be of relevance to God. His guidance through love transforms, changes, empowers, and leads us to places we never imagined we would get through, let alone discover, in our lifetime.

The God Who made the universe and everything in it is the Lord of heaven and earth. He doesn't live in shrines made by humans, and He isn't served by humans as if He needed anything. He gives everyone life, breath, and everything they have. From one man He has made every nation of humanity to live all over the earth. He has given them the seasons of the year and the boundaries within which to live. He has done this so that they would look for God, somehow reach for Him, and find Him. In fact, He is never far from any one of us. Certainly, we live, move, and exist because of Him. As some of your poets have said, 'We are God's children.'" (Acts 17:24-28)

So many of us seek a presence of something that's more than abstract in our spiritual lives. Whenever we talk about faith, spirituality, and the things of God, they seem far-off and distant. God's in heaven, Jesus is at the right hand of the Father, and our blessings are coming from some netherworld region beyond what we can see, right now. Sometimes we need the now more than we need the distance, and that is where faith enters the picture. As faith is the substance (stuff) of that which we hope for, the evidence (proof) of what we do not see, faith gives us a sense of belief and hope, right now, because by faith, we know that God is with us, not just off in heaven, somewhere far away. As we are led by God, we come to this powerful, important, and life-changing realization.

Throughout this book, we have discussed the different things we must employ to be usable by God as well as different things we must deconstruct and rebuild upon to have a solid foundation of spiritual movement. In this last chapter, we are going to look at how God leads us, and we can recognize God's leading, once we have our spiritual foundation.

GUIDING US WHEN WE LEAST EXPECT IT

When we think about being led by God, we think immediately of the concept of people being led to do big, important, grand things. Maybe we think of a missionary hearing God's voice and moving halfway around the world to walk in deep snow and cold to spread the Gospel in an unknown land. We think of a minister being called to start a church. We think of a civil rights activist making a grand protest statement against the establishment that perpetrates wrongs. We don't think of being led by God in our everyday, ordinary lives; somehow, we believe God leaves us to our own devices unless it's some big, monumental task. This isn't true of God at all. God's presence is there to help us through things big and small, and God is with us just as much in the boring and seemingly inconsequential aspects of one's life.

The Lord may give you troubles and hardships. But your teacher will no longer be hidden from you. You will see your teacher with your own eyes. You will hear a voice behind you saying, "This is the way. Follow it, whether it turns to the right or to the left." (Isaiah 30:20-21)

As you tune in to the guidance of God, there are two things you'll probably notice. One is learning how to hear from God, as we discussed earlier. One or more of those different methods of divine communication will become even more real to you, and you will be quick to embrace them and receive those words in your life. The second thing you will probably notice is just how frequently you sense that presence and word within your life. You will start to notice God's guidance in a bunch of little ways, leading you as you seek to make decisions and come out on the other side of better ones.

This is not just about decision making or making better choices, although that is definitely a part of the process and something to embrace. It isn't God's will for us to remain confused, confounded, and always leading down the path of negative choices. What is most important in this is realizing the way that God is always with us. We talked earlier in this book about becoming a part of eternity. Embracing the guidance of God in a bigger sense proves just how much eternity is a part of our right now. There are many groups and religions that teach a lot about the afterlife as a part of eternity, but they don't teach about eternity in the here and now. Finding God's direction for you as an individual, right now in your life, is a powerful and important experience because it directs toward eternity. Instead of worrying about our immediate issues, God's guidance gives us a sense of Him that is beyond what we can see, feel, or understand in the natural. Eternity is a grounding point, an existence that is both within and outside of time and brings us back to wherever we need to be, right now. The issues we have will pass, but God will still be there. Whatever we are supposed to do and however we are supposed to do it is grounded in eternity, rather than running from temporal to temporal. The guidance of God grounds us and takes us to a spiritual understanding that is far beyond anything we can imagine. We might never be rich, or famous, or have all the material wealth we seek, but the guidance of God gives us something we cannot buy; God's presence. By embracing His guidance, we receive Him in our lives in an intimate sense. We know He is there, we love Him, we receive His love, and we are willing to follow Him, even if we don't always understand it.

DRAWN TO ALL THE WRONG THINGS

There it is again…the flesh. I'm sure you are tired of hearing about your flesh by now, and I'm sure you know it isn't my favorite topic to address. The flesh demands we deal with ourselves. Unfortunately, it'll never go away, this side of heaven. On one side, it is a reminder of humility. Our flesh is there to remind us how much we need God. We aren't God, we can't save ourselves, and our flesh's missteps remind us of this fact. The counter part of this is that we consistently need God's grace and the Spirit to remind us of the right way to go and draw us away from all those things that aren't good for us.

When I mention "things that aren't good for us," I'm not talking about the list of sins that most churches have or even a list we might try to compile from reading the Scriptures. Yes, sin is an issue for us; sin is a part of the world of the flesh. There's no denying the grave and serious issue that sin causes us, both spiritually and in the immediate world. What I am referring to here is the way in which it always seems like we are attracted to the things we shouldn't be doing, those that derail us and get us off track.

I know that nothing good lives in me; that is, nothing good lives in my corrupt nature. Although I have the desire to do what is right, I don't do it. I don't do the good I want to do. Instead, I do the evil that I don't want to do. Now, when I do what I don't want to do, I am no longer the one who is doing it. Sin that lives in me is doing it.

So I've discovered this truth: Evil is present with me even when I want to do what God's standards say is good. I take pleasure in God's standards in my inner being. However, I see a different standard at work throughout my body. It is at war with the standards my mind sets and tries to take me captive to sin's standards which still exist throughout my body. What a miserable person I am! Who will rescue me from my dying body? I thank God that our Lord Jesus Christ rescues me! So I am obedient to God's standards with my mind, but I am obedient to sin's standards with my corrupt nature. (Romans 7:18-25)

No matter what is going on in our lives, it seems as if there is always a distraction. We want what someone else has. We want to go somewhere other than where we are. We desire to obey God, but disobedience seems easier or more desirable. Someone else makes a great suggestion or has done something that's really sensational result-wise for them, and we think we should do the same thing. Many times, we start chasing other voices and influences that aren't God, and they may not be bad things; they are just not things that are for us.

Back when I was first doing open broadcasting and podcasting as an apostle, I was one of only a handful of women who were frontrunners as female apostles online. There were a total of five of us: my apostle, the woman who became my apostle later in time, two other women who we knew were out there but weren't real connected to our group, and myself. In those days, it was customary to take on many projects and internet personas, promoting every single thing that any one of us could do. The two leaders I was connected to both had separate podcasting stations, video podcast channels, blogs, and private social networks for their main ministries, women's ministry, counseling, substance abuse, human rights, Bible school programs, mental health, and physical fitness. They also both had at least four or five websites apiece between them all, trying to advertise different aspects of their ministries. They would spend most of their time broadcasting between their different audiences and maintaining their followings in all those different places.

Over time, many of their works tapered off. It was a lot to maintain so many different programs, blogs, broadcasts, and websites, especially given there is only so much to talk about when something is a part of one's work rather than its whole focus. This would go on for a while, and then they would announce a whole new idea and vision, one that would now take center stage. They would focus on it then, for a period. About every six to eight months, their central focus would change. Broadcasts would stop, blogs would abruptly end, websites would come down, and something new would rise in its place.

When they started out, these women were leaders in their broadcasts. They had hundreds and thousands of views because their material was solid and interesting. Nobody was broadcasting on the internet in the same way that they were. Yet when they lost interest in what they were doing or it wasn't what they wanted to do anymore, they would abandon the audience that was exclusively interested in that one aspect of their abilities. This led to many failures in their ministries, including the inability to clearly identify and maintain their audience. In the end, most of those early women faded into the background, with very limited followers, and even less of a scope.

The reason they never went anywhere is simple: they allowed themselves to be distracted by what they wanted to and what they felt was right to do instead of being led by God as to what to do. Any time they saw someone else doing something that seemed to work well for them, they'd jump on board and construct their own version of that work. This is not the way that we should do things, nor is it the way that leads to success in any practical matters. It led to an extensive amount of wasted time and energy, and it was, just simply, not where they were supposed to be (at least in the way they were doing it).

As they were traveling along, Jesus went into a village. A woman named Martha welcomed Him into her home. She had a sister named Mary. Mary sat at the Lord's feet and listened to Him talk.

But Martha was upset about all the work she had to do. So she asked, "Lord, don't you care that my sister has left me to do the work all by myself? Tell her to help me."

The Lord answered her, "Martha, Martha! You worry and fuss about a lot of things. There's only one thing you need. Mary has made the right choice, and that one thing will not be taken away from her." (Luke 10:38-42)

Martha and Mary are often spoken of in terms of having "women's issues." Martha is seen as culturally domestic and extensively busy, while Mary forsakes cultural demands to listen to Jesus teach. Teachers and preachers often pit Martha and Mary against each other, but I don't know if such is fair, nor do Martha and Mary just represent "women's issues." Martha and Mary are a powerful example of what happens when situations come along to distract us, aiming to get us away from where we need to be (seeking the guidance and instruction of Christ). I'm sure had Christ asked for a drink or something to eat, Mary would have been happy to get it for Him. Since He didn't ask, she knew the best thing she could do was avoid the distraction of trying to please Him in a cultural sense (the sense of what she'd been told to do) and just receive what He offered her instead. Martha was distracted by everything anyone had ever told her she needed to do for her guests, and she was worried people would think she was a bad hostess if she didn't do things just right. Martha proves that anything can be a distraction, including cultural expectations (like Martha experienced), embittered emotions, personal ambitions, or reaching for things are simply not for us, no matter how good they might seem to be.

We need to stop chasing our distractions. We stop chasing them when we hear from God, follow His guidance, and start taking the guidance of God seriously, as more than just a nice idea we follow throughout our lives to help us feel better about ourselves. God's guidance is real, and while yes, we might need to try a few things out, it doesn't lead us to skip around every so often to do something new. God encourages us to be consistent, sitting and listening at Christ's feet, so when it is time to get up and do what needs to be done, we can do it.

Assessing Ourselves Properly

There's a spiritual fact that many of us try to avoid. We like to blame the devil and scream and stomp when things just don't seem to go the way we want. There's a part of us that wants to fit in and blend in with everyone else, and that means we desire their successes. We avoid our failures and sometimes our true successes, because neither helps us fit in with those around us. Whether we want to hear it or not, God speaks to us in both our successes and our failures, but we frequently refuse to listen.

Repeat after me: There is room for more than the few things we think are trendy. It seems as if we all do the same things all the time because that's what everyone else is doing. If we are listening to everyone else, we aren't doing things that are God-led. If we aren't God-led, then we can't expect things to turn out the way we hope they will. God speaks to us in what we do well; He speaks in what we don't do well. What we do well doesn't have to look like what everyone else does well, and we need to listen when we just aren't a right fit for something. It's all right to be different. It's all right to have different interests and a different perspective. It's all right to do the things that God has graced you to do, because there is room for those things to be done.

One thing I learned from my former leaders and colleagues that I mentioned earlier was how to be very busy doing things. They were not good models of the examination needed to consider if we should be doing the things we do. They were leading me, but they weren't leading me as to how to hear from God and discern for myself where He wanted me or what He wanted me to do. I was also good at filling my time and being busy, although I took on far fewer projects than the rest of them did. I persisted with the few that I had, and when those seemed to do all right, I started adding other projects that also imitated some of the ones they had. I thought doing women's ministry meant having to have a bunch of women's conferences and councils. I spent an extensive amount of time and money trying to pursue things that helped me to fit in better with my ministry friends and leaders. On the surface, my ministry didn't look that different than anyone else's. I avoided certain topics in preaching, I heralded a certain outlook that imitated other ministers, and I often behaved in the same angry, hostile way many of them did, as well.

It's only been the past couple of years that God really sat me down and had me look at many of the things I was doing…but more importantly, why I was doing them. Most of them were producing little to no fruit at all. I spent my days being busy, doing things that had no point and were not doing anything to enhance the ministry or my own life, in the least. I was aggravated with the people I dealt with on a regular basis, and I felt like I was playing a part rather than being whoever God created me to be. Through a period of four years, I moved farther away from what was comfortable and familiar to me and closer to the heart of God, learning to discern His will instead of glossing over His voice with that of others.

Whatever you do, do it wholeheartedly as though you were working for your real master and not merely for humans. You know that your real Master will give you an inheritance as your reward. It is Christ, your real Master, Whom you are serving. (Colossians 3:23-24)

Discerning God's direction requires us to focus in on what we do for Him, not for the praise and attention of other people. What we do does benefit others, but we aren't doing it so others will like us, praise us, or want to connect with us out of a sense of sameness. Our walk with God does not exist to compete with every other person out there who is also a believer, even if what they do is like what we do. God's desire for us is that we would seek Him and spend our time in pursuit of those things which He has appointed us to do, rather than wasting time in so many fruitless and futile things that take our time, money, effort, and attention away from where we should be.

We need to esteem ourselves properly. We need to know what we are good at, what we are not good at, and recognize the gifts, talents, and abilities that are God-given within us. Following God's will gives the opportunity to use those things for His glory and follow His heart, uniting ours to His. It's a terrible shame to forsake our abilities because we are trying too hard to be like everyone else out there. It doesn't matter how many we have or what they are, because there are no greater or lesser gifts. There is no partiality with God, and it is the work of God that we do and Christ that we truly serve.

MAKE ME A SERVANT

Everybody likes the idea of being "great." What that means might be different to different people, but nobody likes the idea of just being a "nobody." We like to think that what we do makes a difference, and that is the whole reason why we desire to be used by God to begin with. Yet what we might think denotes greatness is probably quite different from what God thinks denotes greatness. If we are going to be great, how does God require us to be great?

We must become as a servant to be usable by God, yet most people balk at the idea of service. Service is considered demeaning, whether it's in the job sector (such as wait staff or housekeeping) or when it is done for the Kingdom. So many ministers avoid the principle of service, requiring others to serve them in various ways that are both unbecoming and frequently offensive. Being "the boss" or working in a field where one gives orders instead of having to take them is considered prestigious, and in contrast, those who must take orders are considered demeaned, and sometimes subject to abuse. The dream lifestyle of many is to give orders and be served, rather than having to be able to do service.

Then the mother of Zebedee's sons came to Jesus with her two sons. She bowed down in front of Him to ask Him for a favor.

"What do you want?" He asked her.

She said to Him, "Promise that one of my sons will sit at Your right and the other at Your left in Your Kingdom."

Jesus replied, "You don't realize what you're asking. Can you drink the cup that I'm going to drink?"

"We can," they told Him.

Jesus said to them, "You will drink My cup. But I don't have the authority to grant you a seat at My right or left. My Father has already prepared these positions for certain people."

When the other ten apostles heard about this, they were irritated with the two brothers. Jesus called the apostles and said, "You know that the rulers of nations have absolute power over people and their officials have absolute authority over people. But that's not the way it's going to be among you. Whoever wants to become great among you will be your servant. Whoever wants to be most important among you will be your slave. It's the same way with the Son of Man. He didn't come so that others could serve Him. He came to serve and to give His life as a ransom for many people." (Matthew 20:20-28)

In New Testament times, the Jews had a concept of the Messiah as being a mighty and powerful king. To them, His main purpose was overthrowing the larger-than-life Roman government. They were occupied and they believed the answer to their political and social discomforts was force (additional violence). Jesus, therefore, came and challenged every notion they had about His role. The result was controversy in the figurehead of His being. Even among His closest disciples, Jesus' role wasn't fully understood. To clarify this, Jesus Himself stated that He didn't come to be served. His purpose was not to mirror those attitudes, ideals, and leadership approaches that were already a part of the world and pervasive within society. Jesus came to do things in a different way: He came to serve.

In ancient cultures, servanthood was associated with slavery (the Biblical word for a servant is the same as slave) or the jobs that nobody else wanted to do, because they were represented with servile work. There were different reasons why someone might have been a slave, as slavery was a part of an economic system, that of debtors and borrowers. Someone might have become a slave because they owed a debt to someone else and labor was the way they would pay off that debt, as a prisoner of war, a child sold into slavery to satisfy a debt, inherited servanthood, and in some instances, as criminals. Slaves might have worked any number of jobs, including tutors to children, farm or physical labor, household work, or executive positions (such as work for a governing official). We might associate these works of service as menial, not all servanthood was regarded as such, and there were many times when a slave's debt was paid and they were free to go, but they decided to stay with their owners. There was no shame in serving; it was honorable work, and many slaves were considered trusted individuals, performing a necessary task in a household or estate.

There was one job that nobody wanted to do, and that was washing the feet of household members and guests. Washing the feet of others was considered a sign of customary hospitality. People wore sandals (not shoes) if they wore anything at all, and most did not bathe daily. This means feet were dirty and dusty, and tracking in all that dirt and dust was unsanitary. People in Middle Eastern cultures also ate reclining on the floor (they still do in most of those nations today), so having dirty feet would have destroyed the enjoyment of a meal. It was the position of one of the household servants to wash the feet of guests in the home as a sign of welcoming and hospitality. If this was not done, it was considered a sign of disrespect, as if you did not regard that guest in one's home.

Can we understand why nobody wanted to do this? Who in the world wants to be up close and personal with someone's dirty feet? It was considered demeaning to have to do this, and it was done out of obligation (because it was someone's job) rather than out of a sense of honor or anticipation.

So, what is the example Jesus gives us for service?

Before the Passover festival, Jesus knew that the time had come for Him to leave this world and go back to the Father. Jesus loved His own who were in the world, and He loved them to the end.

While supper was taking place, the devil had already put the idea of betraying Jesus into the mind of Judas, son of Simon Iscariot.

The Father had put everything in Jesus' control. Jesus knew that. He also knew that He had come from God and was going back to God. So He got up from the table, removed His outer clothes, took a towel, and tied it around His waist. Then He poured water into a basin and began to wash the disciples' feet and dry them with the towel that He had tied around his waist.

When Jesus came to Simon Peter, Peter asked Him, "Lord, are You going to wash my feet?"

Jesus answered Peter, "You don't know now what I'm doing. You will understand later."

Peter told Jesus, "You will never wash my feet."

Jesus replied to Peter, "If I don't wash you, you don't belong to Me."

Simon Peter said to Jesus, "Lord, don't wash only my feet. Wash my hands and my head too!

Jesus told Peter, "People who have washed are completely clean. They need to have only their feet washed. All of you, except for one, are clean." (Jesus knew who was going to betray Him. That's why He said, "All of you, except for one, are clean.")

After Jesus had washed their feet and put on His outer clothes, He took his place at the table again. Then He asked his disciples, "Do you understand what I've done for you? You call Me teacher and Lord, and you're right because that's what I am. So if I, your Lord and teacher, have washed your feet, you must wash each other's feet. I've given you an example that you should follow. I can guarantee this truth: Slaves are not superior to their owners, and messengers are not superior to the people who send them. If you understand all of this, you are blessed whenever you follow My example." (John 13:1-17)

For Jesus to wash His disciples' feet, with a good attitude and encouraging us to do the same, is important. If we are a part of Him (alluding to the washing of baptism, being baptized into His death), then we have part of Him and must be willing to do for others…even when it's menial and unglorified. We look at the crucifixion through the lens of the resurrection today, and how incredibly triumphant our Savior was over death. On Good Friday, the work of a servant wasn't so glamorous and didn't feel so meaningful; it didn't just feel like death…it was death. The same is true for our service work today. It might be honored at times, but it doesn't feel fun; it unites us to Christ in His death. And if we aren't washed of Him, we have no part of Him. If we are not willing to unite in His death, we will have no part in His life, either.

Sometimes we are tempted to take the parts of the Scriptures and the work of Jesus out and about because we like those aspects of Christ best. We like His teachings telling us to be kind to others and about the forgiveness of God, but we don't like the realities of being told to do what He did. Peter is an example of this: he missed the point of Jesus' words and example by being asked to be washed in his body, including his hands and feet. Many of us are constantly seeking more spirituality, more answers, more depth, but once we get it, we don't do much with it. We can't experience Jesus and not experience the service of His walk. We won't ever develop the spiritual insights we seek if we are unwilling to serve.

How do we approach service today?

- We look for ways to be of service to others
- We approach service with a good attitude, recognizing it unites us to Christ
- We don't avoid the work that seems menial
- We uphold service as an honorable aspect of our spiritual lives
- We don't judge different forms of service
- We don't expect service to be all about us, but about God

Be Still...And Let Go

The cares of this world can fill our minds. Questions about both natural and spiritual things can keep us up at night. We can wonder about the things of God in excess. We can try to figure out how to handle our own lives, discern more about our call, even try to reconcile the things we see in Scripture or in church history that don't make sense to us. We can spend periods of time questioning our faith when ethical aspects of it don't measure up with what we expect or perceive today, and this can cause us to experience personal tumult.

I want to say that I don't think it is sinful to have thoughts or questions about your faith, your spiritual life, the history of spiritual things, or about God. We don't learn if we don't ask questions, and having questions is not a sign of weak faith or faltering faith. Questions and thoughts are a sign that you are growing spiritually and that you want to know more about your faith. We run into trouble when we find our questions unanswered or degraded by others, and this can cause us to think God rejects our questions and our ideas. This isn't the case, at all. God doesn't reject the questions we have, as we can see from the example of Job. Throughout Job's incredulous trial, he gained insight into the wisdom of God and the depths of human experience. Job learned it's not the answers that are the problem, but the way that we formulate our questions and thoughts. As we process with God, it's not wrong to have those thoughts or questions, but when we grow in God and gain a deeper spiritual insight, we will see our questions and musings through a different light.

There will forever be things in the Scriptures and church history that we dislike or don't really understand well. This is because the Scriptures, as we understand them today, were written thousands of years ago in a different culture that we can and can't relate to, both at the same time. We can relate to ancient culture because it was full of people with issues, feelings, and emotions that aren't that different from how we might think, feel, and process today. At the same time, we don't always understand all the cultural nuances and societal issues that those who wrote the Bible encountered. They saw their relationship with God through their experiences (much like we do today). Yes, that means some of that influenced how they saw their spiritual lives. It doesn't mean they didn't leave the door open for different interpretations and understandings to come, but it does mean that we relate, and sometimes we don't relate. Sometimes understanding takes more work than other passages, and we don't always readily like or relate to everything spiritual that we experience.

Last night I was watching television and came across an old episode of *The Johnny Carson Show*. There were three guests on the episode, and I had no idea who any of them were. In his monologue, Johnny Carson made jokes about the Carter administration, of which I was not even alive at that point in time. I didn't understand what he was saying, nor the dialogue with the guests, because the whole setting of the show was before my time.

Reading the Scriptures and trying to understand God through this lens can be like my experience watching that old television program from before my time. I can relate to political humor and excitement over celebrity guests that the people were able to learn more about. I know what a big deal Johnny Carson was in his day, and how many people got their start on his show. The nuances of the program, however, I missed. I don't understand why the political humor was funny and I don't know who the guests were. There are things I don't understand because my frame of reference isn't the same as the frame of reference in the show. The same is true when we try to gain insight into a frame of experience we don't easily understand.

Let go of your concerns!
Then you will know that I am God.
I rule the nations.
I rule the earth. (Psalm 46:10)

We should study; we should learn; and we should also be still and let go of what we don't understand. There will forever be things we don't like or don't understand within the same frame of reference. Unfortunately, we can't eliminate the things we don't like or understand. Those are things there that are a part of another person's (or group of people's) experience and while it might not apply in the same way for us now, we can learn from them as people. We can ask our questions and seek our answers, but we should never forsake knowing everything for the knowledge of resting secure in Christ and knowing God is a part of life.

Somewhere in here we start to see faith as a solution, rather than the problem of understanding. We don't need to know everything, and we don't need to see everything through our immediate lens to embrace our history. We can still serve. We can still believe. We can still know. Maybe not in the same way that people did once upon a time, but we can know, for ourselves, right now. We can let go of our cares, our worries, our fears, our misunderstandings, and we can embrace Who God is, for ourselves, right now, so we can serve and love Him all the days of our lives.

DISCERNING SEASONS

We've all heard someone say, "God's time is not our time." If you study spirituality for any period, you will find this fact to be very true. We like to think of God operating on a timetable, a line of history, if you will, where He does this, and this happens; if we do this, God moves; if this happens, then that will happen. Many clever slogans and chants of the church attempt to place God on our timetable, making us feel better about our own efforts and periods of waiting. The reason this doesn't work is because God's "time" isn't really time. We live in time that is measured like a timeline, with a beginning and an end, and God lives outside of this time, in eternity. This is why our relationship with God calls us to become a part of eternity, to develop a different understanding of time and our experiences.

The ancients had a better understanding of eternity than we do because they learned from watching nature. They didn't have clocks or watches and weren't as time-bound as we are today. Their lives lasted as long as they did, and there wasn't always a huge push to accomplish so much in one's lifetime. People's lives were prescribed for them back then, and those outlines were much simpler and quieter than today. People didn't see the world open before them, forced to meet various standards and challenges to find their place in the grand scheme of things. The ancients watched day pass into night and night pass into day, they watched the seasons change, they watched prophetic cycles come in circles and had a view of time that was circular rather than linear. They realized that things have a way of coming around again; testing us, trying us, changing us, and revealing to us. Times and seasons themselves come and go in one's life, for a period that is at the Lord's discerning. We come in one way, and we go out another. If we missed the answers, we could find them again on the next go around. That's the brilliance of times and seasons. It's also totally contrary to how we see and regard time.

In our view of time, things are either past, present, or future. That which is past is over, that which is present is now, and that which is future isn't yet. In eternal time, everything simply is. We are existing and dwelling for the glory of God, and that which is past has a way of coming around again while that which is future has a way of transforming our present. In eternal time, we find a way to discover hope. In endings are new beginnings; in new beginnings are new starts; in eternity, it all equates to different cycles that go on, are ongoing, are transforming, and are purposeful, all within their own ways.

Everything has its own time, and there is a specific time for every activity under heaven:

a time to be born and
a time to die,
a time to plant and
a time to pull out what was planted,
a time to kill and
a time to heal,
a time to tear down and
a time to build up,
a time to cry and
a time to laugh,
a time to mourn and
a time to dance,
a time to scatter stones and
a time to gather them,
a time to hug and
a time to stop hugging,
a time to start looking and
a time to stop looking,
a time to keep and
a time to throw away,
a time to tear apart and
a time to sew together,
a time to keep quiet and
a time to speak out,
a time to love and
a time to hate,

a time for war and
a time for peace.

What do working people gain from their hard labor? I have seen mortals weighed down with a burden that God has placed on them. It is beautiful how God has done everything at the right time. He has put a sense of eternity in people's minds. Yet, mortals still can't grasp what God is doing from the beginning to the end of time.

I realize that there's nothing better for them to do than to be cheerful and enjoy what is good in their lives. It is a gift from God to be able to eat and drink and experience the good that comes from every kind of hard work.

I realize that whatever God does will last forever. Nothing can be added to it, and nothing can be taken away from it. God does this so that people will fear him.

Whatever has happened in the past is present now. Whatever is going to happen in the future has already happened in the past. God will call the past to account. (Ecclesiastes 3:1-15)

The Scriptures specifically state that God has placed eternity within us, in our hearts, giving us a sense of it amidst all the things that come and go in this life. There isn't just one time of life, there are also opposites; and still then, longer and longer lists of things that come and go, change, and modify us. Eternity transforms us; God embraces us; and we embrace God. We reframe time when we start learning about times and seasons, which are periods of time that last within the realm of eternity. We might feel them in chronological time, but their measure is beyond what we understand here. We always have the promise of hope, blessing us, because if something doesn't seem right, it will only be that way for a time and a season. Once that passes, if we don't get it right, we can trust that something, at some time, will come around us again and captivate us into a new change, a new outlook, next time around.

Life doesn't make sense without God. We have this sense and perception of eternity, but we don't understand it if we do not have the work of God alive within us. If we recognize our times and seasons, we have a deep indwelling of God's hope as He directs us to what is always best.

THE CENTER OF HIS WILL

Centering ourselves in God's will means we decrease ourselves – our flesh, our own personal selfishness, control issues, wants, desires, and the feeling that we must have things our own way – and come into a better place, an eternal place, where we align what we've always sought with what God seeks and desires for us. If this sounds a lot like what we've discussed previously, it bears repeating. We can think we are doing God's will and totally miss the mark, because we haven't sought to center ourselves in God's will and make it so that whether we move to the right or the left, the top or the bottom, that God's will surrounds us on every side.

We tend to miss the will of God because we worry about our feelings and thoughts of a situation instead of centering God's will in the middle of it all. We don't consider if God has called us to do something. If it doesn't appear to benefit us in some obvious way, we assume God might not be in it or that the devil is working against us, trying to make things difficult for us. We assess the will of God by our desires, which can make God's will seem self-driven from the outset. This distortion of the will of God eliminates our growth from the spiritual equation, an aspect of the will of God that is often very relevant and important. We can't be so caught up in our feelings, emotions, and concepts all the time that we keep missing the will of God and, therefore, make judgments and calls based on things that can change and fade as quickly as they rise and cause us to feel a certain way. Sometimes God calls us to do things we would rather not do, because those are things that help us to grow and see His will from a different perspective. It is those places of challenge that challenge us to cut through those feelings and emotions, and start embracing the will of God for real, because we learn those things are temporal, and passing away, while the will of God gives us a heads up for the eternal picture.

Living in the will of God is deeper, however, than just doing things we don't like. When we are in the will of God, we discover a divine alignment with Him that helps us to unite with Him. It's not about us anymore and what we want or don't want but uniting our will to His to find the place of wholeness. Walking in the will of God is about salvation as a process, walking towards any level of perfection that may be possible, even this side of heaven. As we work toward that ultimate goal, our will purposes and merges into His, and we walk toward the good purpose of God, without hesitation.

My dear friends, you have always obeyed, not only when I was with you but even more now that I'm absent. In the same way continue to work out your salvation with fear and trembling. It is God Who produces in you the desires and actions that please Him.

Do everything without complaining or arguing. Then you will be blameless and innocent. You will be God's children without any faults among people who are crooked and corrupt. You will shine like stars among them in the world as you hold firmly to the word of life. Then I can brag on the day of Christ that my effort was not wasted and that my work produced results. My life is being poured out as a part of the sacrifice and service I offer to God for your faith. Yet, I am filled with joy, and I share that joy with all of you. For this same reason you also should be filled with joy and share that joy with me. (Philippians 2:12-18)

If it's your heart to be a good representative of the Gospel, you need to be a good disciple of God's will. A hard, undeniable truth we like to ignore about the Christian life is that it's not an easy walk. The world doesn't readily understand it and we don't always understand what God is doing through us or wants to do within us. Being a believer and properly representing the Gospel requires the constant, deliberate action to die to oneself and obey God instead. When we follow the will of God, we find the road that leads to true life. We don't just embrace a boring, purposeless existence, but one that leads us to significance. We can see our purpose here, and our purpose in the world to come, all mapped out within God's will.

Discovering the will of God is an unfolding journey that takes us to places we'd never imagine and things we'd never considered for ourselves. We don't have to be super-spiritual, avoid life, or jet off to a foreign land and mediate many hours a day. The will of God is accomplished within us when we walk in the life He has called us to live. No matter how ordinary our lives may feel, we can achieve a deeper understanding of His will as we walk and live our lives. We will grow to see both supernatural and simple things, the ways in which God works for us that are obvious as well as those ways that are subtle, and all bringing it to a place of realization as we see God move on our behalf, time and time again.

ACCEPTING THE CHALLENGE

It's a great thing to be a Christian. It's great to read the Scriptures, even every day, if that's what you want to do. It's great to go to a solid church that helps you understand and learn more about God. It's great to be led by great leaders, and to love our leadership. It's great to read Christian materials and learn about the ways of the faith. All these things are fine, and good, and part of the lives of millions of believers worldwide…but they aren't enough if they don't lead us somewhere. Being a Christian should mean something more than just being a part of a religious denomination. Reading the Scriptures shouldn't be a task, much like finishing a great novel. Going to church should never become an obligation. Leadership should teach you about God's will and learning to follow His leading. Reading Christian materials should educate, not merely entertain or confound. All of the things we do in the Christian life should take us to something else, lead us to a deeper place, and form and shape our hearts for the spiritual work that God has for each and every one of us, having a heart He can use for whatever it is He wants to do within each of us.

I want to issue a challenge to you, the reader of this book. Look over your life and ask yourself, "Am I just going through the motions?" Before your answer is no, look a little bit more carefully at what you do and all the hopes and dreams you have had for your life at different points in time. There are things you desired to do that God placed within you that you have since abandoned because they seemed impossible, too hard, or someone told you that you couldn't do them. Maybe there's even something right now that you can't see your way to quite do because you don't understand how to bring it to pass.

When we are a part of eternity, we are able to gain insight into "time" from a spiritual perspective, but that doesn't change the fact that, right now, as we live in this life, we all have so much time to do the things we are appointed to do in this lifetime. We thank God for second, third, fourth, and fifth chances and beyond, but doesn't God give us many opportunities so we can finally get it right one of these times? Isn't that something we would like the ability to do, is know we did what God desired for us to do, and acknowledge that desire as our own? Don't we all want to know more of how to do this thing where we rest in His will and our lives change and transform?

Dear friends, don't ignore this fact: One day with the Lord is like a thousand years, and a thousand years are like one day. The Lord isn't slow to do what He promised, as some people think. Rather, He is patient for your sake. He doesn't want to destroy anyone but wants all people to have an opportunity to turn to Him and change the way they think and act. (2 Peter 3:8-9)

Your cycle will come around again, to go through the process discussed in this book and embrace each and every part of it as you delve deeper into the heart of God to transform your own. This time, no matter what stage of this process you are on, take it. Take it and receive the cleanness of heart that God gives to those who seek His will as their own and transform. Let the Spirit of God fill you and the grace of God bless you. Rest in all that God desires you to have and all He desires you to become. Find that place of blessing, because heaven's interventions only come through as we are willing to place ourselves within them.

<u>A LESSON FROM RUTH'S LIFE</u>

The book of Ruth is not one that is commonly studied in church. I don't think most understand its contents. They regard it as a nice story (maybe suitable for a women's conference) rather than a life-changing message. A summary of the story of Ruth is as follows: Ruth was married to a man from Moab when tragedy struck, leaving her husband, brother-in-law, and father-in-law dead. The women remained: Ruth, Ruth's mother-in-law, Naomi, and Ruth's sister-in-law, Orpah. Orpah decided to go back to her own people to resume her life, but Ruth made the difficult decision to commit to the care for her mother-in-law, Naomi. This was not customary, especially given the two of them had no provisions for life and no way to care for themselves. Regardless, Ruth saw her way to devote herself to her mother-in-law, bound by the direction of God for her.

Then Naomi said to her two daughters-in-law, "Go back! Each of you should go back to your mother's home. May the Lord be as kind to you as you were to me and to our loved ones who have died. May the Lord repay each of you so that you may find security in a home with a husband."

When she kissed them goodbye, they began to cry loudly. They said to her, "We are going back with you to your people."

But Naomi said, "Go back, my daughters. Why should you go with me? Do I have any more sons in my womb who could be your husbands? Go back, my daughters. Go, because I am too old to get married again. If I said that I still have hope. . . . And if I had a husband tonight. . . . And even if I gave birth to sons, would you wait until they grew up and stay single just for them? No, my daughters. My bitterness is much worse than yours because the Lord has sent me so much trouble."

They began to cry loudly again. Then Orpah kissed her mother-in-law goodbye, but Ruth held on to her tightly. Naomi said, "Look, your sister-in-law has gone back to her people and to her gods. Go back with your sister-in-law."

But Ruth answered, "Don't force me to leave you. Don't make me turn back from following you. Wherever you go, I will go, and wherever you stay, I will stay. Your people will be my people, and your God will be my God. Wherever you die, I will die, and I will be buried there with you. May the Lord strike me down if anything but death separates you and me!"

When Naomi saw that Ruth was determined to go with her, she ended the conversation. (Ruth 1:8-18)

We like to romanticize the story of Ruth (especially when it comes to Boaz), but if we study the text in depth, there is no justification for such a fanciful understanding of the words. Ruth had to have a divine conviction and trust God for what was done in her life, because it must not have been easy for her to make such a powerful decision. She had to work hard in physical labor, in the social status of a pauper. She had to spend her time with Naomi, who wasn't always the most pleasant person in the world to be around. Naomi had experienced tremendous loss and was out of sorts, unhappy, melancholy, and angry. Life dealt with her an unfair hand. She didn't expect a better day or any more of a gracious promise to come and lighten the rest of her life. Then we add to the mix that Ruth literally had to throw herself at Boaz, because Boaz had no interest in marrying her, whatsoever. Even that might have raised some questions within her, as I've heard it said that Boaz was around 40 years her senior! Even right up to the point where Ruth forced the issue, Boaz was looking for another relative to get him out of things! What Ruth had to do was dangerous. It wasn't fun. She also went through a painful and lasting loss, one that filled her mind in quiet hours. She probably wondered why she was doing these things and why this had to be her station, at times. Yes, in the end Ruth was blessed, but there was a whole lot more in the middle that didn't feel like blessing — it felt like work, like "What in the world did I get myself into?!"

Ruth proves to us that being led of God is not an easy process, but it is a necessary one if we want to position ourselves for the blessing God has for us in our lives. She wasn't out trolling for a man or looking for anything extraordinary in her life to get her out of her situation. Ruth went about her life, minded her own business, worked hard, rose to the challenges, and stayed close to the things she knew that she had to do. It might not be the fairy tale we hope for, but it proves to us that doing what God has for us to do will bring us to the fullness of God's will, every time.

PRAYER
TO HAVE A HEART GOD CAN USE

Create a clean heart in me, O God,
and renew a faithful spirit within me.
Do not force me away from Your presence,
and do not take Your Holy Spirit from me.
Restore the joy of Your salvation to me,
and provide me with a spirit of willing obedience.
(Psalm 51:10-12)

Father God,

I come before You today and pray in earnest that You would create in me a clean heart, that would open the door for a renewal of right spirit within me. Lord, I want to receive more of You and more of Your Spirit. Let me embrace Your grace. Help me to do the hard work of self-examination, motive, and ultimately, change in my life. You know where You want to take me and I want to go, even though I don't see the whole way right now. I want to be able to reach out to people with Your love and Your purpose. It is my earnest prayer that my life would be a living testimony, full of prayer, spiritual insight, seeking Your face, and learning how to be still and trust in You when I don't have all the answers.

Restore Your joy within me, not the happiness of this world that fades and passes, but a true sense of joy that comes from experiencing Your salvation, and willingness to follow You. I know change only comes from You, the One Who never changes, because as I transform, I will understand more of Who You are and the greatness that you have for me in Your spiritual reality of eternity.

Show me, Lord, where I can serve. Show me, Lord, what I need to do and know to get from here to there. I am Your willing vessel. Take my heart and transform it to be more like Yours, that I may have a heart You can use, rooted firmly in the center of Your will.

In Jesus' Name I pray,

Amen.

RELATED WRITINGS
BY THE AUTHOR

- *Calling the Kingdom Remnant: A Journey Through the Book of Haggai* (Righteous Pen Publications, 2015)

- *Fruit of the Vine: Study and Commentary on the Fruit of the Spirit* (Righteous Pen Publications, 2015)

- *Rubies & Pearls: One Hundred Days for Change* (Remnant Words, 2017)

- *Seeds for the Season: 91 Days of Breakthrough* (Righteous Pen Publications, 2018)

ABOUT THE AUTHOR
DR. LEE ANN B. MARINO, PH.D., D.MIN., D.D.

These that have turned the world upside down
are come hither also.
(Acts 17:6, KJV)

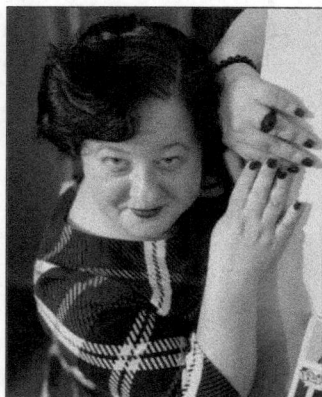

DR. LEE ANN B. MARINO, PH.D., D.MIN., D.D. (she/her) is "everyone's favorite theologian" leading Gen X, Millennials, and Gen Z with expertise in leadership training, queer and feminist theology, general religion, and apostolic theology. She has served in ministry since 1998 and was ordained as a pastor in 2002 and an apostle in 2010. She founded what is now Sanctuary Apostolic Fellowship Empowerment (SAFE) Ministries in 2004. Under her ministry heading Dr. Marino is founder and Overseer of Sanctuary International Fellowship Tabernacle (SIFT) (the original home of National Coming Out Sunday) and The Sanctuary Network, and Chancellor of Apostolic Covenant Theological Seminary (ACTS).

Affectionately nicknamed "the Spitfire," Dr. Marino has spent over two decades as an "apostle, preacher, and teacher" (2 Timothy 1:11), exercising her personal mandate to become "all things to all people" (1 Corinthians 9:22). Her embrace of spiritual issues (both technical and intimate) has found its home among both seekers and believers, those who desire spiritual answers to today's issues.

Dr. Marino has preached throughout the United States, Puerto Rico, and Europe in hundreds of religious services and experiences throughout the years. A history maker in her own right, she has spent over two decades in advocacy, education, and work for and within minority spiritual communities (including African American, Hispanic, and LGBTQ+). She has also served as the first woman on all-male synods, councils, and panels, as well as the first preacher or speaker welcomed of a different race, sexual orientation, or identity among diverse communities. Today, Dr. Marino's work extends to over 150 countries as she hosts the popular *Kingdom Now* podcast, which is in the top 20 percentile of all podcasts worldwide. She is also the author of over 35 books and the popular Patheos column, *Leadership on Fire*. To date, she has had five bestselling titles within their subject matter: *Understanding Demonology, Spiritual Warfare, Healing, and Deliverance: A Manual for the Christian Minister; Ministry School Boot Camp: Training for Helps Ministries, Appointments, and Beyond; Discovering Intimacy: A Journey Through the Song of Solomon; Fruit of the Vine: Study and Commentary on the Fruit of the Spirit;* and *Ministering to LGBTQ+ (and Those Who Love Them): A Primer for Queer Theology* (and its accompanying workbook).

As a public icon and social media influencer, Dr. Marino advocates healthy body image (curvy/full-figured), representation as a demisexual/aromantic, and albinism awareness as a model. Known to those she works with, she is a spiritual mom, teacher, leader, professor, confidant, and friend. She continues to transform, receiving new teaching, revelation, and insight in this thing we call "ministry." Through years of spiritual growth and maturity, Dr. Marino stands as herself, here to present what God has given to her for any who have an ear to hear.

For more information, visit her website at kingdompowernow.org.

www.ingramcontent.com/pod-product-compliance
Lightning Source LLC
LaVergne TN
LVHW051057080426
835508LV00019B/1927